Days and Nights at The Second City

Days and Nights at The Second City

A Memoir, with Notes on Staging Review Theatre

Bernard Sahlins

 Ivan R. Dee   Chicago

Library of Congress Cataloging-in-Publication Data:
Sahlins, Bernard.
    Days and nights at the Second City : a memoir ; with Notes on
staging review theatre / Bernard Sahlins.
        p.   cm.
    Includes index.
    ISBN 1-56663-431-8 (alk. paper)
    1. Sahlins, Bernard.   2. Theatrical producers and directors—
United States—Biography.   3. Second City (Theater company)—
History.   I. Sahlins, Bernard. Notes on staging review theatre.
II. Title.

PN2287.S225 A3 2001
792'.023'092—dc21
    [B]   00-065760

For Jane

Contents

"We are born to be tragic in our fate,

lyric in our feelings, but comic

in our behavior."—George Santayana

Preface

As the English say about cricket, the theatre is not a matter of life and death, it is much more important than that. We come and we go, but the words of Sophocles and Shakespeare echo on.

For me it started in the eighth grade in Chicago when I put on a short play for the class. I was hooked. While it wasn't exactly the same epiphany that felled Luther as a young man, it certainly was memorable—especially when, having always had trouble differentiating lower-case h's and k's in my printing, I distributed handwritten programs listing my offering, to the class's great amusement and Miss O'Brien's consternation as a short shit.

As to the theatre itself, it was, and remains, astonishing and thrilling to me that one can put words on a page that can be translated into concrete actions that seem real and can move audiences to tears or laughter.

Yet while I have long been enthralled by the theatre, most of the productions I have seen fail to measure up to my dreams as a thirteen-year-old. I have since concluded that, for one, theatre is a most difficult art form. Start out with a good play, excellent cast, fine director—and much of the time it still does not work. Perhaps my printing error was closer to the mark than I realized. Nevertheless, hope springs. Every once in a while, as an audience member, one sees a work so transcendent as to change one's life forever— every once in a while.

But transcendent or not for the audience, for the practitioner the theatre is truly a vocation. It is one of those activities, like the priesthood and medicine and law should be, in which life and work become one, in the service of what is perceived to be a worthy goal.

Yet in my case, after the eighth grade, except for a small role as a bearded villain in a Sunday School play, I retired from the theatre. For more than twenty years I kept my hand in by attending plays and serving on the boards of failing theatre companies. Then, in my mid-thirties, I bit the bullet and, with Paul Sills and Howard Alk, founded The Second City.

The Second City is a theatre presenting short comic scenes about contemporary events and ways of life. Like most theatre ventures, we have had our share of failures. Unlike many of them, we have often been highly successful. If there is a primary purpose in writing about it, it is to set down for others something of what has been learned in creating and living with such an institution.

For somehow this tiny venture quickly became an important phenomenon in the recent history of theatre, heralded for its contribution to popular entertainment. Early on it achieved some measure of national, even international, recognition, and many members of its casts—the Belushi brothers, Bill Murray, Gilda Radner, Harold Ramis, Alan Arkin, Joan Rivers, John Candy, and many, many others— went on to successful careers as actors, directors, and writers. One reason is, I believe, that we never thought of our-selves as popular entertainers.

Paul Valéry famously said, "Everything changes but the avant garde." Of all the arts this probably holds truest for the theatre, many of whose fledgling practitioners, rather than seeking to learn from history, can hardly wait to teach the past where it went wrong. Unlike painters who learn to draw and join to the past the lineaments of their own time; un-like musicians who learn harmony and add their contempo-rary discords—actors and directors emerge each year from our drama schools with little interest in or knowledge of past tradition, no belief in it as something that steadily evolves, no sense of incorporating the new in the matrix of what has so long been gathered. Instead they are ready to revolt vig-orously against what they do not know. As a result, every twenty years or so one sees the same defiant attempts to break down the fourth wall and "make it really real."

This wasn't true of us, the founders and the cast of The Second City. We were university people, imbued with respect for intellectualism and the great masterworks. We had all served our apprenticeship in the classical theatre. We knew that "realism" in our time is different from the realism of ancient Greece or of Victorian England or even of America in 1920—that realism itself is a style, a relative term. We knew that stage reality is not the reality of everyday life. We held with Fellini when he observed, "If I want reality, I'll go outside." We believed in a theatre of strong texts and honest acting.

Yet we were still young enough to want to change the world and to believe that we could. We were influenced by Brecht and by what we had read of the German cabarets, and we wanted to make our statement—though years later it was John Bird, the English satirist, who supplied us with the properly ironic line: "After all, it was those little satiric cabarets in Germany in the thirties that did keep Hitler out of power."

Yes, we were seriously "of the theatre." We had cut our teeth on plays of every period. Some of us truly qualified as intellectuals. Others of us could pull off credible masquerades as such. Our emphases were always on the art form: on truthful acting, solid structures, intelligent choices. Luckily we started in a period when Brecht, the WPA Theatre, the European cabaret tradition, and the political situation had brought the popular theatre closer to the classical theatre. We caught a current and were swept along to a certain amount of notice by the world.

What follows is not a formal history. It is, in part, a personal story about the first twenty-five of Second City's forty years (to date), one thread in a tapestry of historical events. It is also a how-to book for those who are interested in the form, setting down what I learned in producing and directing The Second City. I have tried to convey a sense not so much of what we saw and did but of what we thought and felt, as well as something of what we learned.

In the course of remembering this past, there are events and people I will surely but inadvertently omit. As I say, this is a memoir. I don't have the best memory for facts, and if I've misspoken, or omitted mentioning people in spite of outside checking, that is why. I apologize for my forgetfulness to those I left out.

Some years ago I led a series of directing workshops at The Second City from which I have drawn much of the material for notes on staging that accompany this memoir. I hope they will be useful to those interested in staging review. Some twenty directors, actors, and writers attended. Their alertness, intelligence, and skepticism play no small part in whatever virtues their portion of this book exhibits.

Finally I wish to thank all the directors, actors, musicians, and staff with whom I worked at The Second City. I think of them all with great affection.

Days and Nights at
The Second City

1
The Beginning

In 1576, James Burbage erected a wooden theatre in Shoreditch, a sleazy section of London. It was the very first of the English public theatres. Burbage came out of the small artisan and middle class in England. He united in himself the trade of carpenter and the profession of actor, and he built a building—such as had not been seen in England before—designed for the practical purpose of providing a permanent home for a company of actors. He called it simply "The Theatre."

In the course of his planning, while figuring out how to organize his project, Burbage made what is arguably among the most important contributions—if not the most important—to the theatre world ever made by one man. To prove that I do not say this lightly, weigh the fact that some twenty years later, in a company headed by James Burbage's son Richard, one of the company members was an actor—and, incidentally, a playwright—named William Shakespeare. You can see that when I so value James Burbage's contribution on a comparative scale, I do so quite seriously. What he did—like so many important discoveries once they have been achieved—seems simple now. But it really was revolutionary. He did nothing less than invent the box office.

Up to the time James Burbage came up with his idea, players would give their performance in a field or in a castle hall or public square. At the end they would bow and start to pass the hat, only to find that the audience had melted away. Burbage had another idea. Build a special place to present drama and charge the audience a penny *before* the performance. Brilliant. To this day, theatre managers, staff, and casts should, every night before curtain time, offer up a small prayer to James Burbage. His ingenuity changed forever the structure of dramatic presentation.

Thanks to Burbage and his discovery, there followed in England a veritable orgy of public theatre-building. Elizabethan London was unique in Europe because of its many theatres. Like Burbage's playhouse built of wood and able to accommodate thousands of people, these theatres were the wonders of foreign visitors. All this from the notion of a box office.

While the material advantages of Burbage's concept are clear, even more important are the spiritual implications of his work. When Burbage installed the box office, he not only changed forever the structure of play presentation but—and here is the delightful and wondrous point—he started the process of transforming the actor from being a beggar, who humbly passed the hat, to being an artist, who was held to be of some worth to the community. For me Burbage represents the indispensable, the crucial role of the artist-entrepreneur: to bring to art the world's respect and to the artist, self-respect.

April 1959

Several of us, Chicagoans, mostly in our early thirties, many of us graduates of the University of Chicago, had worked together as actors, directors, and producers in many theatres for many years. We had presented plays ranging from the classics to new works still in manuscript. In some good weeks we had earned the princely sum of seventy-five dollars—in some weeks.

Some years ago the Japanese director Tadashi Suzuki described to me the regimen imposed on his actors, which included sweeping the stage before each rehearsal as an act of artistic purification. "We too did that," I said. "We too swept the stage—in fact we cleaned the entire theatre, not for artistic reasons but out of economic necessity since we couldn't afford a janitor." I never thought to make it a requirement for artistic achievement.

Now, in 1959, we were tired of the start-up-in-hope-and-go-down-in-flames cycle. We were pushing thirty and beyond. We decided to start another kind of theatre, we hoped a "popular theatre." We weren't aiming to "sell out," just to bend a little. Besides, there was a vaguely egalitarian virtue in working with popular forms that suited our politics.

It wasn't an entirely new idea for us. We had tried something like it in bars and showrooms around town. We took as our model those experiences plus some vague ideas of European cabarets, and dim memories of the *Living Newspaper* and the *Pins and Needles Review* done during the Great Depression by the WPA Theatre. We were especially influenced by Brecht and by what we had read of German cabarets. Although we were a bit undecided as to the exact form, it was a point of honor not to compromise our skills and intellect.

May 1959

The corner of Wells Street and Lincoln Avenue, a stone's throw from bustling, downtown Chicago, was in one of those lonely areas that circled the busy center of industrial cities in the era before gentrification. There we found a couple of storefronts at an affordable rent, which we hoped eventually to turn into a cabaret theatre. A mile and a half south of us lay the Loop with its great stores and office buildings. A short distance east was Lake Michigan and the city's Gold Coast, and a mile north sprawled the trendy Lincoln Park neighborhood. Earlier in the century the area had provided the warehouses and distribution centers where trucks unloaded produce and supplies for the rest of the city. Now it was quiet, even desolate—small shops in old buildings, some rooming houses, a few Edward Hopper bars.

When it came to local theatre production, Chicago in 1959 was a barren scene. Except for the Goodman Theatre, the major theatrical activity was provided by touring shows originating in New York, supplemented by a few summer theatres in the suburbs. Attempts at resident theatres had been few and short-lived. Now we were to embark on yet another.

December 16, 1959. 7 p.m.

The usual Chicago winter cold. If we were lucky, we thought, there might be an audience of twenty or thirty for the open-

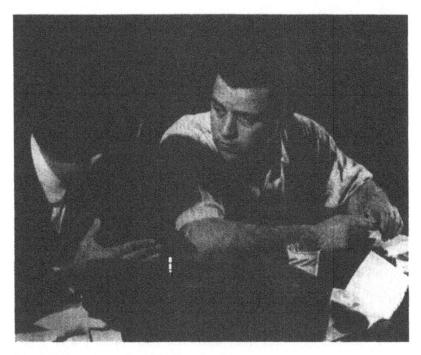

Paul Sills at work with the first company.

ing night of our new theatre, which we called The Second City. Hadn't we failed often enough to now?

Three of us devised and founded The Second City. Paul Sills, a matchless director with a longtime interest in improvisation, was a golden boy—attractive, articulate, gifted, charismatic. He was barely thirty and had directed dozens of plays from every period. Paul is several kinds of genius. As a director he has that rare faculty of inhabiting each moment as it is born on the stage. Any slight deviation from the truth, any flash of uneasiness that arises from a false note—which for most of us is a passing, forgettable twinge— is for Paul an excrescence to be furiously excised. The wonder of it all is the way he carries out this operation. Although normally highly articulate, when it comes to conveying information to an actor he rushes to the stage emitting strange, incomprehensible grunts and burbles, meanwhile reinforcing with violent and seemingly random body language the message he bears. Lo, by some miracle of communication, the actors understand precisely what he wants to convey, and the rehearsal goes on. No false moment is allowed, no shortcuts. The fact is that Paul, like Chekhov, hates "acting" and loves truth. Anything hammy or affected is anathema to him.

In his work and in his person, Paul radiates idealism. He is a theatrical pied piper, inviting his actors to embrace the purest, highest ideal of the art and of themselves as artists, then leading them in a crusade against the Philistines. That is why some high-priced stars gladly work with him for a pittance.

I learned to direct from watching Paul Sills. I was never able to match the total effectiveness of his incoherence, but I did learn to detect what I now call "the awful fiction." This is when a character in a play does not notice, or pretends not to notice, something that is happening on stage until long after that character should have noticed and the audience already has. For example, a husband comes home from work sporting an air of gloom that would do justice to Cassandra. His wife greets him at the door and asks how his day went, as if he had entered normally. A simple "What's the matter?"—a question that every audience member is already asking—would propel the scene forward.

Howard Alk, our pipeline to the counterculture, couldn't act, play the guitar, or sing, but he managed to do all those things convincingly. Howard was a great bear of a man with a highly developed sense of irony, a voracious appetite for high-level gossip, and a well-developed nose for trends and fakery. Howard stayed with us only a few months and then went off to do whatever his thing was; but his incisive knowledge of young, avant-garde thinking was invaluable at the start.

And myself, Bernard Sahlins, fascinated with the theatre and now, having sold my share in a tape-recorder factory, retired though not rich, in my mid-thirties. We three had met at the University of Chicago four or five years earlier and had tried various theatre projects which had succeeded critically and failed financially. Now we and many of our actor colleagues were at loose ends. But I was the only one among us who had not committed to the theatre as vocation. I had only dabbled in it, often and intensely, but never totally. Now I was leaving the world of business (where I never felt comfortable) for the world of theatre. It took me a decade to feel I belonged, to achieve a level of comfort with my new life.

December 16, 1959. 8:30 p.m.

As I say, we would have counted ourselves lucky had there been twenty people at the opening. But a half-hour before curtain time there were more than a hundred. Our capacity was one hundred twenty. Over the years at least five hundred of that one hundred twenty have introduced themselves to me, claiming to have been there on opening night.

We three had not come together to build a theatre. We had been burned enough times doing that. This was still the time of the Beat generation, and we started out to found a coffee house where we idlers, including the actors whom we had worked with for years, could loll around and put the world in its proper place. We pictured ourselves there, drinking coffee and listening to poetry with a few of our friends, sort of a San Francisco Beat scene in Chicago. It is hard to imagine now, but in Chicago then there was no "scene" for theatre aspirants: few places to work, almost no way to earn a living.

We searched the Near North Side for a location and found two adjacent storefronts. One had housed a hat shop, the other a Chinese laundry. Both of these enterprises had foundered, and the stores were empty. In the case of the Chinese laundry, the exit must have been precipitous: for several weeks after we took occupancy, people would knock and mournfully enter brandishing their laundry tickets. We were unable to help since Wong Cleaners & Dyers had left no forwarding address.

The rent was cheap because, despite its nearness to downtown and to the Gold Coast, this was hardly a high-traffic area. (Since then that section of Wells Street has flourished, first as a honky-tonk collection of bars and night spots, now as a trendy avenue with five coffee houses, four Italian restaurants, and the city's best cigar store within two blocks.) We hired a couple of itinerant carpenters and sat back to await the opening of our coffee house. But after a little while we grew restless. Maybe we ought to stage some sort of show.

People like Studs Terkel, who had participated in the WPA Theatre in the 1930s, recalled doing a "living newspaper," that is, reading from a current newspaper and commenting on, even dramatizing, the news. This inspired us to think again of a topical review in a setting where the audience could drink and smoke—a cabaret in the European sense. Hadn't we played with the review form in previous ventures at other people's bars? Why not a cabaret of our own, with music and songs and scenes and blackouts? After all, we were already building the coffee house. We already had plans for tables and chairs and drinking and smoking. All we needed was a small stage. Certainly we had plenty of out-of-work classical actor friends to choose from. Most of them were hovering about before we hammered our first nail.

"Why don't you get a job?" We all heard that, from our parents and some of our friends. Work and life were balanced differently in those days. Older people (in their forties) remembered the Great Depression: the fear and misery of being out of work, the desperation. Considerations like "quality of life" were luxuries, perhaps dangerous to dream of. Blake's "I sometimes try to be miserable so I can do more work" found ready assent from our parents. But by 1959 a long period of affluence led to a rejection of these fears. The young were ready to fly.

"The theatre? That's no life," sniffed my mother. "You should stay in the tape-recorder business." True, I wasn't quite as fancy-free as the others in the project. After all, I was a school generation older. I admit to a kind of shock at the fact that many male and female students were cohabiting as a matter of course, and that sex and travel and life decisions, the way young people loved and lived in 1959, were more casual than I was used to. Life wasn't that free when I was a student. We had to work hard to get laid. By today's mores it was all rather tame, but not to me at the time.

In other ways too, though I did my best not to show it, I was a fish out of water. My role with theatres had always been that of patron or adviser or even cheerleader. I looked at actors and directors across a divide, fascinated, distant, and a little bit awestruck. Although I had been involved with these very people for years, I had never committed to that life. Now I devoted my days and nights to it. Now what had been a game was suddenly serious. I had traded a secure livelihood for the uncertainties (and the pleasures) of art. I did see it that way. But for a long time I belonged to neither world. Was it a Faustian bargain? I pretended to be at ease, but I never stopped peering at myself in this new life.

Our first company included Barbara Harris, Severn Darden, Mina Kolb, Eugene Troobnik, Andrew Duncan, Roger Bowen, and Howard Alk. A short time after we opened, Bowen and Alk left. Alan Arkin, who as a youngster had studied with Paul Sills's mother, Viola Spolin, and Paul Sand, who had studied in France with Marcel Marceau, replaced them.

The Dream Team: Our First Cast

Partly by chance, partly by selection, the first Second City cast—intelligent, well informed—displayed a range and variety of talents that meshed like the gears of a fine watch. In skill and attributes they so complemented each other that they served as casting prototypes for years. A polymath Severn Darden type was sought avidly, as was a witty, pretty Barbara Harris type, a deadpan Alan Arkin, an affable Andrew Duncan. Of course we never found clones, but we did wind up with great variety in small compass.

Andrew Duncan. There is a reason that successful talk-show hosts command such high salaries. The ability to speak to an audience about everyday things in one's own person seems easy but is difficult, and rare. In all my years at The Second City there have been only three or four actors who could master this feat. Andrew was the first and perhaps the

The original Second City cast: (left to right) Eugene Troobnik, Barbara Harris, Alan Arkin, Paul Sand, Bill Matthieu, Mina Kolb, Severn Darden, Andrew Duncan.

best. This was especially important at the beginning, when the rule was to introduce most scenes in direct address to the audience. Solid, not flashy, instantly ready to play Mr. Average Man, Andrew was an invaluable cast member. To him belonged the parodies of those official voices that blare at us from our radios, our television screens, and the public part of our daily lives.

Eugene Troobnik. He of the mellifluous voice. He was close to embodying the stereotype of the classical actor but self-aware enough to parody the type brilliantly. Invaluable at playing senators, executives, and generals, Eugene is best remembered in a parody of Superman, doffing his shirt to reveal the logo of "Businessman"—"able to leap loopholes at a single bound."

Severn Darden. Sui generis in 1959 and not duplicated since. The legendary Severn, scion of an old-line Southern family, was a stocky, tallish man with a vacuum-cleaner mind that I swear retained and could instantly call forth every obscure fact, philosophical tenet, and literary work ever produced by man. And whether in his famous art lecture devoted to explaining a blank canvas ("Featuring two shades of white in which both shades are exactly the same ...") or in his scene as Oedipus Rex ("It's not my fault"), Severn could juxtapose all this information to devastatingly comic effect.

In his personal life too, Severn was the stuff of legends. The most famous concerns the night when he, together with his date, managed to enter the great gothic Rockefeller Chapel on the campus of the University of Chicago. Alerted by the sound of unauthorized organ playing, the campus police, advancing down the aisles, were treated to the sight of Severn throwing himself across the altar and screaming, "Sanctuary! Sanctuary!"

Barbara Harris. Barbara, who went on to a distinguished career on Broadway and in film, was the innocent-looking ingenue with the unexpectedly rapierlike mind. She combined accurate analyses of middle-class ridiculousness with a stellar acting talent to skewer the would-be bohemian suburbanite or the self-styled intellectual. But what set audiences back on their heels were the moments in an otherwise richly comic scene when, through the magic of her acting talent, they glimpsed a serious and emotion-rich inner life.

At a Chinese restaurant, Mina Kolb and Eugene Troobnik (front) are the hapless diners; Alan Arkin (left, rear) is the truculent chef and Paul Sand the waiter.

Mina Kolb. Mina was, in the best sense of the word, a clown. Although she came from a rich background in commercial TV and was the one cast member without extensive experience in theatre, she more then held her own with her deadpan comic insights into the minutiae of everyday life.

Alan Arkin. If one were to meet Alan in ordinary circumstances, the last guesses one would make about this serious, somewhat taciturn man would be that he is a superb actor and a talented musician—performer, singer, and composer. (Alan wrote the famous "Banana Boat Song" and a great number of comic masterpieces, including "I Like You Because You Don't Make Me Nervous.") Alan is intense and relaxed at the same time, with a deadly sense of humor. Like many great actors, he has a superb talent for mimicry. After a moment of study he can walk like anybody, talk like anybody, and sing like anybody.

Howard Alk. Although not a professional actor, Howard, a co-founder of The Second City, had a firm grip on what the counterculture was thinking and saying. He served as a balance wheel to our tendency to be awed by the intellectual and was quick with the witty analysis of life's contradictions. It was he who defined a Freudian slip as "meaning to say one thing and saying a mother." Howard quickly tired of acting and was replaced by Alan Arkin.

Roger Bowen. He of the devastating wit (he conceived the Businessman sketch for Eugene Troobnik) also quickly tired of the eight-shows-a-week grind and was replaced by Paul Sand.

Paul Sand. Sweet Paul Sand. If mime were a popular art form, Paul would be a major star. He was physically eloquent, riveting when playing a fish in our underwater ballet, touching when responding to the instruction from a phonograph record entitled, "Make-a-Friend."

Bill Matthieu. A piano was an indispensable part of the show as we conceived it, not only to accompany songs but to underscore and to play scenes in and out. We were for-

Severn Darden (front) improvising as Avery Schreiber plays the guitar.

tunate in meeting with Bill Matthieu (later known as Allaudin), a great musician who could parody any style on the spot and was sensitive enough to know when not to play.

By September the theatre was shaping up, though between moonlighting carpenters and the natural propensity of show people to start their day at suppertime, I was groggy for many weeks. My biological clock took a long time in adjusting. All my working life I had been hard at it by eight in the morning. Now things began to stir only in mid-afternoon.

I was constantly reminded of the story about Ferenc Molnar, the Hungarian playwright living in Vienna at the beginning of the twentieth century. Molnar rarely went to bed before 5 a.m. and accordingly woke in the afternoon. One day a friend prevailed on him to be a witness in a court case, which is how Molnar found himself driving in a carriage through the streets of Vienna at the unlikely, ungodly hour of 8 a.m. He was amazed, had never seen anything like it. The bustling streets were filled with people and vehicles—going to work, making deliveries, rushing to appointments. Who were these people? Puzzled, Molnar turned to his friend. "Tell me," he asked, "are they all witnesses?"

Eventually I did adjust.

Naming Time

Naming the theatre was a collective endeavor that took weeks. Each day we and the actors would gather and offer the gems we had thought of overnight. The short list occupied four single-spaced pages.

At about this time a series of articles about Chicago, entitled "The Second City," was appearing in the *New Yorker.* As the appellation implied, their author, a wonderful journalist named A. J. Liebling, did not think much of our metropolis on the lake. In fact he was relentlessly negative about its citizenry and its culture. I think it was Howard Alk who suggested we defiantly carry the title of the articles as our banner. It was one of those "of course" moments.

Thus it was: Paul directing, Howard on stage, and I taking care of the rest. Most of the people we worked with were University of Chicago graduates, and the audiences, in our heads (and indeed, the majority of the real audience for our

first six months), were made up of university students and
faculty. They shaped our reference levels, our characters,
our causes, and our humor.

We took the summer and fall of 1959 to ready our space,
with our moonlighting tradesmen working away at the theatre, with our cast playing theatre games, and with Jimmy
Masucci designing our space. A couple of engagements in
our past theatre life had taken us to St. Louis. There a handful of bar and club owners in a Victorian area of the city
known as Gaslight Square had embarked upon a frenzy of
Victorian restoration—gilded chandeliers and mirrored bars,
antique storefronts and botanical prints. Here was an odd
sidebar to the taste of the times. While we, together with
the venturesome, liberal club owners in St. Louis and the
new breed of entertainment entrepreneurs in Chicago, embraced "modernism" culturally, we were retro in our visual
tastes. Political rebellion was in, but when it came to design, plush Victorian nostalgia was cool.

At the design center of the St. Louis renaissance was a
most remarkable figure. With very little formal education
and no background in interior design, but with an incredibly inventive talent, Jimmy Masucci, a tall, thin, shambling
man, became the guiding design genius of Gaslight Square.
Jimmy was not the most articulate of men, but his taste was
unerring. In St. Louis he not only found the antiques, he
created the most fetching environments out of the most unlikely elements. We hired Jimmy, and what did he do? He
bought telephone booths, which then consisted of four wooden
panels, each some seven feet high, the top halves of which
were glass. He painted them black and paneled the walls
with them. In the center of each, under the glass, he in-

stalled prints from a set he had cut from a book on Roman antiquities. The effect was stunning, especially when highlighted by the electrified gas lamps extending from the walls and some jerry-built red velvet banquettes, all well within our meager budget.

By mid-November 1959, Paul and the cast had worked out a group of disparate scenes, songs, short blackout pieces, and parodies. Paul's mother, Viola Spolin, who taught theatre on the West Coast, had over the years developed a series of theatre games designed to teach acting and the development of material.* Paul started with her *Theater Games* and from these gradually developed a full-fledged review. Later I found that we, all unknowing, were working in a tradition that started in 600 B.C. with the short comic scenes arising from the Greek harvest festivals. In any event, we produced an hour and a half's worth of unconnected scenes and songs that we ourselves were not quite sure how to organize.

It wasn't as though we were reinventing the wheel. At the University of Chicago and in several ventures we had experimented with short scenes developed through improvisation, and we were happy with the individual pieces that Paul and the actors and Bill Matthieu had developed. But we felt there was something missing. We tried imposing a unifying theme, a rudimentary plot, but nothing seemed satisfactory.

For a year Mike Nichols and Elaine May had been the darlings of the New York scene. They came from our group, and success had descended on their two-person show with

---

*Her books on theatre games have been an invaluable source for theatres and schools and have remained in print for many decades.

Two of the stalwarts from the first Second City company, Paul Sand and Barbara Harris.

the intensity and suddenness of a hurricane. We called Mike and asked him to come to Chicago to give us a critical appraisal—we would pay his fare, of course—and he did. He looked at what we had and suggested we stop trying for a connection. The joy of the work, he said, was watching a skilled ensemble playing a great many roles and displaying a range of talents for singing, miming, acting, and nimble witticisms. That, he said, was all we needed. And if we needed time between scenes, it would be an asset for the actors cleverly to introduce the next scene either in character or in their own person.* Don't change the scenes, he advised, don't add any structures, don't impose a theme. Stay with what you're doing.

We cheered. "By gosh! The man is right! How sensitive, how persuasive—how easy!"

It was years later when I realized that artistically we had upset the normal pattern of theatrical evolution. The classical theatre, in its brief flarings and long dyings, had ever looked to the popular theatre for actors and stagecraft. We reversed the process. From the theatre of Shakespeare, Brecht, Sophocles, and O'Neill, we brought what we knew to the popular theatre. We lived by the classical theatre watchwords:

—Respect your audience by playing at the top of your intelligence.

—Assume they are at least as smart as you are, if not smarter.

—Respect every character you play, even the darkest villain.

—Play all characters from within and never be superior to them.

---

*The introductions became a popular part of the shows. We introduced almost every scene with carefully prepared, funny, and illuminating texts. As the years went by, with the acclimation of the audience to the quick cuts and transitions of film and TV, the introductions became fewer, then nearly disappeared.

—Bring every bit of your talent to the stage.

—Tell the truth.

Between June and December we had lots of time to discuss the deep philosophical issues of how close the tables should be, what kinds of ashtrays we should have, and what sort of coat-check system we should use. The committee on plumbing made its urinal recommendations, and a management decision was made not to compose a manual for our wait staff.

Fortunately I was too busy to second-guess my decision to embrace the life of the theatre. Had I looked up for a moment and thought about our dwindling finances, I would have panicked.

Meanwhile, we bought one hundred fifty bentwood chairs at auction for a dollar apiece, cobbled together tables with black Formica tops on cast-iron bases, equipped a bar and a kitchen from a bankrupt restaurant, and covered the whole place with carpeting left over from business conventions at a dollar a yard. We hung a few stage lights (purchased used) over the small platform that was our stage. There was an untouchable, active gas pipe running floor to ceiling, upstage left. (The gas pipe remained as long as we occupied the space.) Our only scenery consisted of six of the bentwood chairs. We were equally parsimonious with costumes, deciding that only the elements of costume were compatible with our vision. An army jacket was enough to suggest a general; a white coat, a doctor; a fedora, a gangster. We had plenty of spectacle frames without lenses, hats galore, and some bad wigs. We dressed the men in brown corduroy suits from Brooks Brothers and the women in black dresses.

November 1959: Enter the Mafia

Winter came early. In late November, just before we opened, a tall man in a grey fedora appeared. He wanted to talk to the "boss." With the three of us assembled, he announced that he was there to "help" us by seeing to it that we would have no "trouble" from unruly patrons or "undesirable elements"—which he assured us we would have if we didn't choose to use his services. Furthermore he offered us two ways of paying for this arrangement. We could either give him a percentage of the business or pay him a weekly fee. He spoke softly. He mispronounced words. The delivery, the syntax, and the implied threat came right out of a bad B-movie. For a moment we thought it was a hoax. Then we knew it wasn't. We didn't know whether to laugh or cower under a table. "Here," continued our benefactor, "is my phone number. Think it over." At the door he turned. "I'll be back next week if I don't hear from you." That was scary.

After a quick powwow we decided to fight. We called the police and our local alderman, who was reputed to have some influence in certain circles. A policeman showed up with a large book of photographs, and we were able to make an identification. We were not reassured when the policeman pursed his lips and said, "Hmm!" We heard nothing for two weeks. Then on a Sunday morning we were summoned to the theatre. Our plate-glass front had been shattered by a bottle of the most foul-smelling liquid, which was spilled all over our lobby. It took us two days to get rid of the noxious smell. Three weeks later the same thing happened. After that I guess we were considered adequately punished. But for many weeks I was wary when walking down dark streets.

Sahlins (left) and musical director Fred Kaz debating a lyric.

Stink bombs aside, in early December we had a theatre, a show, a wait staff, and a bartender. We set our admission price at two dollars and fifty cents, with no minimum for the drinks.

"Excelsior and Other Outcries" was the name of our first Second City show. It was the first of a long series of names that had nothing whatever to do with the contents of the review. Some of my favorites over the years include "Unanimous Raves from All the Critics," "Truth, Justice, or the American Way," "Freud Slipped Here," "Jean-Paul Sartre and Ringo," "I Remember DaDa, or Won't You Come Home, Saul Bellow?", "Orwell That Ends Well."

December 16, 1959. 11:30 p.m.

Our stage lights were controlled by five small dimmers—more like living room than theatre equipment—and they were operated by whichever actor happened not to be in the opening or closing of a scene. On that first night, when the entire company was taking a bow, there was no one left to bring the lights up and down, a situation that none of us had thought of before, and that I realized in the nick of time. I ran backstage and twirled the dimmers through interminable curtain calls. There it was, the delightful sound of people who would not stop telling us they had been moved. We were a hit! We couldn't believe the response. We sat around afterward and drank beer. Over the next few days the four newspaper critics (there were four daily papers in Chicago in those days, now two) confirmed the audience reaction.

Once the papers were on the streets, the phones started ringing. All of us were enlisted in taking reservations. We were now successful artists. What did that mean? Quit our day jobs? Look forward to long-term employment? None of us would go that far. We "knew" from our past experiences that it wouldn't last, and all our friends agreed. We would repeat to one and all the immortal words attributed to a local Chicago impresario, "If they don't want to come, you can't stop them." For many months after that first performance we remained certain that our luck would run out and that no audience would appear the next night. Even if it was a brutally cold Tuesday in February, one empty seat convinced us it was the beginning of the end.*

---

*Today a Second City show will run for as long as six months and often is changed only because everyone involved has had enough.

So we kept things lean. The three "owners" would check the waitresses out after the show and come in during the day to place orders and get things ready for our part-time bookkeeper. And even though we were selling out, we ran our first show just eight weeks. We figured that was how long it would take us to run out of fans.

But what was this show that was causing such a stir, and why was it so exciting? It was—and still is today—a review in two acts, with the actors (generally six in number) playing a great many characters in a great many places, from the president in the White House to the cop on the corner to the housewife in the suburbs. The elements are simple: fifteen to twenty-five short comic scenes, blackouts, musical numbers, and parodies, strung together with no thematic connection. The form was already old in the fifth century B.C., but it is a serviceable vessel into which one can load rich cargoes. Without a set, just a back wall with two doors, without costumes, with just words and our great actors, there is pure theatre magic on that stage.

Contrary to some predictions, having a bare stage in no way diminished our effectiveness. Whether it is a review scene or a play, the impact of a theatre piece, its authenticity, comes primarily from acting and text. It is difficult on a television show or in a movie to portray a living room convincingly with one potted palm and an easy chair. In these media realistic settings are almost mandatory. But for the stage, the old adage that all one needs is "two boards and a passion" is on the mark. I value lighting, costume, and set, but the stage work can succeed if any or all of these are at a functional minimum. It will fail if the acting or the text is deficient. Paul Sills was a stickler for truthful acting and concise text, and that tradition has remained.

The show itself ran somewhere around an hour and forty minutes, including a fifteen-minute intermission. Since we were trained in improvisation but skeptical about its viability as a continuous presentational form, we had decided that the review we presented and marketed would be polished, honed, and more or less "set." But for our own amusement as well as that of the public, after we took our bows for the regular show we took suggestions for scenes from the audience. Half an hour later we returned to do a set of improvisations based on those suggestions. In confirmation of their hit-or-miss character, admission to the improvisations was free.

It took us only a short time to realize that the improvisations had another, very important function. They were the incubator for originating and polishing new material for the next show. As Alan Arkin pointed out, they turned out to be "public rehearsal." Improvisations that were well received were either repeated or worked on in rehearsal and then replayed in the improvisation section. (We were always careful to introduce these as "scenes we are working on.") Thus from the opening night of a show we were already preparing a new show. When it was time for that new show to open, we would have a group of tested scenes ready to go.

Here I want to clear up a long-held misconception. Although we were, and still are, perceived as an improvising theatre, we almost never—except for an occasional "game" within a show and in the free period after a show—used improvisation as a presentational form. For us it was a tool for developing material. Paul Sills and Viola Spolin had perfected the use of improvisation as a vehicle for "writing" scenes. It turned out to be a faster, more equitable method for developing a show, since the actors could use themselves to their maximum ability. In effect, each cast member was a writer.

Part of the attraction of our show was due to the state of the nation. Senator Joe McCarthy was dead, but the shades of his Communist witch-hunt still darkened the landscape. The cold war was in full swing, and while it was not quite a period of repression, there was a certain wariness in the air. Political jokes and topical subject matter were scarce, confined to such enclaves of rebellion as San Francisco. Television featured fluffy sitcoms like "Father Knows Best."

Even at the time, to speak of the decade of the fifties was to evoke images of conformity, of going along, of tract homes and the quest for identity. A corrosive miasma of paranoia and red-baiting still hung in the atmosphere. Not for nothing do we look back on those days as shrill and materialistic—even frightening.

But Allen Ginsberg had read his poem "Howl" in October 1955, and The Second City was part of the expression of a growing anti-establishment sentiment. The sixties, the rebellious sixties, were dawning as a counter to the conformist fifties, and questions were being asked. As usual, literature led the way. Burroughs, Kerouac, and Ginsberg; Bellow, Roth, and Glass; Mailer, Eldridge Cleaver, and Norman O. Brown. In comedy, the careers of Dick Gregory, Lenny Bruce, and Mort Sahl were beginning to be noticed beyond the counterculture. To put Eisenhower and Nixon on stage, indeed to do anything topical, to smash icons, to discuss the events of the day from the points of view of well-acted characters, was deliciously new and terribly exciting for young audiences. We were often treated to the phenomenon of open-mouthed young people, hanging about forever after each show, bedazzled by hearing their concerns expressed on stage.

One of the joys of the review form is its immediacy. A straight play can take years between its conception and its appearance before the public. With a review scene, an idea conceived in the morning can be seen on the stage that night. And one can capture the sometimes ephemeral visit of the *zeitgeist,* reflecting the preoccupations of the actors and the audiences at a given moment in time. The review form is flexible and can stretch to receive even the most abstract of concepts.

A certain amount of oppression is good for comedy. The firmer the taboo, the more excitement when it's violated— like Eve's apple made more delicious by being forbidden. But unlike the Beats, unlike Bruce, we represented the respectable, the acceptable face of dissent. We were neither hostile nor in a rage. We did not separate ourselves from the mainstream. Our irony was gentled by the fact that we included ourselves among its targets. We soon stopped trying to save the world in favor of laughing at it. We did not preach the apocalypse. Our audiences laughed the laugh of recognition.

We were, of course, political liberals. And we took our easy shots at the Ku Klux Klan, at Nixon, at racism. But we also recognized that the proper target of a satirist is himself and the members of his own class, their shibboleths, beliefs, and dogmas. The worthiest scenes exposed our own culpability in the face of such issues as racial prejudice and injustice.

Another reason for our success was not artistic but financial. Mostly through sheer dumb luck we had stumbled on a form, and a formula, that made for economic advantages unusual in the theatre. We had a lower cost base than even a storefront theatre. With no set, with a couple hundred dollars' worth of costume elements, with a small cast, with one musician and a stage "crew" consisting of one combination light, sound, and stage management person, we were lean. There were other savings. We rehearsed a new show with the same cast that played the old one. We earned extra revenue from serving drinks. We never advertised.*

These factors enabled us to keep our prices down. In a business notorious for being transient, we survived and even flourished with a relatively small theatre.

But the chief reasons for our survival, aside from our favorable business setup, were the intelligent actors, highly skilled at both writing and acting, guided by the genius of Paul Sills. Plus the fact that not one of us, including our savvy, loyal waitresses, wanted anything other than a good, uncompromising show. Because we had a bar and served at tables, people often characterized us as a nightclub. To them I would explain that we were a theatre that served drinks, not a bar that put on a show.

That is the sum of it. We appeared at the right time with a great format, a viable financial venture, a great director, and marvelous actors. Although we were and still are known as political satirists, the fact is that politics was but a fraction of the subjects we considered. We often disappointed those who held the idea that we should be more heavily en-

*We depended entirely on feature stories and other free media. Although The Second City now advertises, it did not do so for its first twenty-five years.

gaged in social critiques. But irony was our métier. We applied it to the family, to courting, to work and the workplace. We parodied Mozart and Superman. We sang songs about nature. We were young people talking to young people.

And it didn't hurt that we were inexpensive. We felt from the beginning that our competition was not other theatres but movies, and we always tried to be within a few dollars of the price of a movie ticket. With all that, it was an actor's medium, and it was Paul Sills who held us all to the highest standards of acting.

After a couple of months it became apparent that we were indeed a success. And while it is true that every actor, every director, writer, producer in the theatre expects a miracle each time out, there coexists a pessimism that accepts the many failures. "I must complain," said Swift, "that the cards are ill-shuffled till I have a good hand." And in this business good hands are rare.

No wonder so few, if they do triumph, avoid the perils and pitfalls created by success. I don't mean the obvious discomfort of having one's privacy constantly invaded.* I mean the quietly insidious ways in which the promise of success can affect the work at hand. Guilt, hope, fear, desire: these form a dangerous concoction. As I look back on twenty-five years of The Second City, I see clearly that our deepest problems came from our successes, starting with my co-founders, Paul and Howard.

Howard was a free spirit, chafing at any long-term commitments. His departure was amicable and, as I see now, in-

---

*John Belushi and John Candy would hide out in our offices when they came to Chicago, weary of being accosted by strangers who felt it within their rights to waylay these familiar figures in public. Imagine eating in a restaurant where every eye is focused on your table habits.

The Berlin Wall goes up. Bill Alton (left) as a reporter and Del Close as a right-wing American general at the scene.

evitable. Paul had a more complex reaction. In a most subtle way it was difficult for him to deal with success. In the theatre a production is always a group achievement. Thus, oddly, theatrical success is a leveler. In the theatre the director and some of the actors may have been stars going into a production or may become stars as a result of a production, but custom and indeed reality impose a "we're all in this together" attitude which mandates that success be shared. It wasn't that Paul was greedy or nonsharing; far from it. But somehow success was noisy, disturbing his muse.

Two months after our opening, it looked like we would survive, but Paul's inquietude that had propelled us to this point did not fade. Paul paled at the thought of endlessly doing shows in a single style. The telltale signs of his restlessness were evident. Already he was talking of the Story Theatre form that he eventually staged on Broadway and for television.

This was the first of many times that I found myself trying to keep things together. At that point, if Paul went, we all went. I had a sneaky solution.

In some of our earlier incarnations we had worked with an impossibly talented, impossibly demanding gentleman named Del Close. I sent for Del some six months after we opened. Sensing that Paul was alarmed, even panicky, at the prospect of doing show after show, I thought it might be helpful to have Del Close around if we needed a director. We had worked with Del in the past and had found this acerbic, quick-tongued, excessive man to be a genius, a dark genius—from Kansas yet. When he wasn't astounding audiences with intelligent wit, he was drinking, drugging, and destroying himself. He was the quintessential beatnik—Burroughs, Kerouac, and Ginsberg rolled into one. Del, who died in the year in which this book was written, and I had a long-standing, sometimes good-natured argument about the use and abuse of improvisation. He found in it a magical, transcendent quality that resulted in a unique stage expression. I saw it as a technique, a stage tool like mime or fencing. He maintained that it was indeed an art form, deserving to be elevated to presentational status. I felt that to do so was a self-indulgence, that improvisation elevated to a form of presentation failed most of the time, that any scene could benefit from editing, concision, and shaping.

Del devoted the last years of his life to teaching and inspiring a small, devoted band of committed improvisers. It

Joyce Sloane,
Jewish mother of
us all. [Jennifer
Girard]

was a guru-disciple relationship that bred fervent devotees to improvisation as an almost mystical form of theatrical magic.

On the night before Del died, there was a party in a basement recreation room of his hospital. Dozens of people were there to pay their respects in what was really an affecting celebration, sort of a wake with the central figure alive and present. The party was only slightly marred by the Druid ceremony that closed the evening (Del was a witch). Del himself, white-haired and white-bearded but with impish grin intact, sat there with air tubes and IVs snaking around his wheelchair, clearly enjoying it all. When I approached to pay my respects, he wagged a finger at me and half-bellowed, "It *is* an art form," and then went into what I thought was a long chuckle.

I said, "Del, for tonight it is an art form." Whereupon someone said, "You're standing on his air tube." It was like a bad Second City improvisation. I hastily slid away and all was well again. The next day Del died, having willed his skull to the Goodman Theatre to be used in the gravedigger's scene in *Hamlet*.

Now that I look back on it, I think my bringing in Del might have been a shameless sort of manipulation. But it worked. Del was the spur to Paul's competitive nature. Paul directed another show. Later Del joined the company as an actor, escaped briefly to San Francisco, and then returned to direct. Actors loved him in what I called their "let's eat babies together, send up our parents, and do drugs" mode. Eventually his excesses were unsupportable.

Also rejoining us from previous ventures soon after we opened was Sheldon Patinkin. Sheldon, twenty-four years old at the time, was a prodigy. A talented pianist (he had steered us through a production of the *Three-Penny Opera* when he was nineteen) and opera lover, and widely read, Sheldon, in addition to being an achiever, was also the group's Jewish mother and its priest. He listened to confessions, took no sides, was always available and generous with his sympathy. I hired Sheldon as general manager and general assistant to everybody.

Early in 1961 Sheldon was supplanted—no, augmented—as the Jewish mother of us all by the real article. Joyce Sloane joined us, at first selling benefit performances to small organizations, then taking on a general role as associate producer, a role she filled for me for twenty-five years. Joyce is calm, infinitely loving, and generous as a saint.

Hundreds of actors have appeared on Second City stages over its forty some years, and I swear that Joyce keeps in touch with all of them, remembers their birthdays and their children's names, follows their careers, visits them in New York or California or Toronto, calls, writes, and sends presents. She is universally loved. No small part of her job was to heal the wounded feelings often left by Paul or myself. Nor are Joyce's maternal ministrations confined to The Second City. The entire Chicago theatre community basks in her beneficence.

This, then, is how it was at the start: Howard, Paul, myself, Joyce, Sheldon, Del, a successful show. It was a good beginning, but we had no presentment of how quickly our lives were to change.

2
New York,
New York

Some eight weeks after our grand opening, we opened our second show. One of the newspaper critics created the phrase that was to be repeated by reviewers for the next forty years: "Nice show, but they're not quite as good as they used to be."

Still, it didn't take long for the news to get around. Word of this upstart Chicago company and its success spread through the country's theatrical community and beyond. Soon after we opened we were visited by a delegation from Moscow headed by Madame Furstevenka, then minister of culture. She was accompanied by the novelist Mikhail Sholokhov, author of *And Quiet Flows the Don,* and a Latvian poet whom we dubbed "the captive." He silently glowered throughout our meeting. Madame Furstevenka kept quizzing us about our reactions to American racism, world capitalism, worker's inequality, and so forth. I don't know what she made of our noncommittal responses, but she did refer to us in a subsequent report of her trip that was printed in *Pravda,* calling

us "a young Chicago collective." We rather liked that, but
we weren't sure how the House Un-American Activities Committee would feel about it. Fortunately none of them could
read *Pravda*.

Madame Furstevenka was but one of a steady stream of
celebrities who came to see what the fuss was all about.
Kenneth Tynan, the celebrated English critic, stopped in and
wrote about us. Tennessee Williams came and raved about
a two-person scene centered on a Greek artifact. Both Zero
Mostel and Cary Grant showed up more than once. Woody
Allen, who was doing his stand-up act at a local nightclub
called Mister Kelley's, caught a show, though I'm not sure
if he was as interested in the show as in one of our actresses
with whom he was reputed to be briefly involved. Bette Mid-
ler, fresh from her triumph at a New York bathhouse, worked
out with the cast. So did Tom Hanks, Robin Williams, and
many others.

A notable visitor was Sir Edmund Hillary, conqueror of
Mount Everest, who attended one night with Tenzing Nor-
gay, his Sherpa climbing companion. Despite the fact that
Tenzing spoke no English, he hugely enjoyed the show. I
watched him from time to time, puzzled at his delighted reactions. Afterward he fell into a voluble conversation with
the interpreter. It seems that Tenzing had constructed, from
our unconnected scenes, a complete story, something like
King Lear, about an old king (Severn Darden) and his two
daughters, featuring an unsuitable marriage but with a happy
ending. We thought about it for a minute.

The national press got in the act. "The temple of satire,"
Time magazine called us.

Among the celebrities who made The Second City a
stopover point early on was David Merrick, the great Broad-

way impresario who uncomplainingly stood through an entire show, professionally appreciative of a sold-out house. On and off for the next three months, at his prompting and with the promise of his support, Paul and I made brief journeys to New York, looking for a suitable location to duplicate our Chicago venue. Although all doors opened to us at the mention of David Merrick's name, we could not find a suitable space. But our appetite for a New York appearance was whetted.

Meanwhile we made our first foray into television with a one-shot appearance as one of the "acts" on Hugh Hefner's syndicated show, "Playboy at Night." The stint involved attending several of the weekly parties at the Playboy Mansion. Talk about disconnects—we University of Chicago types wandering among the scantily clad bunnies, inspecting the meandering swimming pool with its underwater views, open-mouthed over the whole sybaritic sweep of it all. We spent much of our time talking to a fellow guest who had shared the TV show with us: a thin, tall, handsome comedian with a somewhat controversial act. His name was Lenny Bruce. He would soon become one of the icons of the counterculture.

Both the television and recording industries were attracted to The Second City, but sales were always disappointing. We made several records over the years, none of which hit the top thousand. We were funny, good actors, and nonthreatening personalities, but the great mass of the public—certainly most people over forty—found us too heady and too obscure to be embraced. Early in 1961, Paramount television conducted the first pay-per-view television experiment, with us as one of the features. They crowded three huge cameras into our little theatre and filmed over several days as we ran through our entire repertory. For some reason the experiment was carried on in Canada, where, in Etobicoke, a suburb of Toronto, we were transmitted to audiences numbering in the hundreds. If we were not a mass attraction in the United States, we were surely a head-scratcher in Canada.

But we were becoming a bit of a cult, and inevitably all the interest we were arousing did not go unnoticed in the talent-agency world. None of the major agencies now have a presence in Chicago, but in the sixties the William Morris Agency ran a three-man operation with offices in the Tribune Tower. The agents were engaged primarily in booking the many nightclubs that still dotted the entertainment scene. Tony Fantozzi, who later became a Morris powerhouse, came to the theatre to see what was up. A week later Harry Kalcheim, a Morris honcho, arrived from the New York office when, as it happened, Paramount was filming. The wild reception we were getting from our audiences, who were doubly excited by being on this still young medium of TV, was infectious. Even for jaded agents we were a fresh attraction and, presto, we were represented.

Harry Kalcheim, one of two brothers high up in the Morris hierarchy, was not the Hollywood caricature of an agent, nor was he jaded. Soft-spoken, sympathetic, gentlemanly— courtly even, he never snapped his fingers once in all the time I knew him. And he genuinely loved our work.

Soon we were introduced to Max Liebman, to us an elderly gentleman in his sixties who had last produced "Your Show of Shows," that great television series starring Sid Caesar and Imogene Coca and written by Woody Allen, Carl Reiner, and Mel Brooks, among others. Harry Kalcheim brought Liebman to see our show. Next day he called us and said he would like to present The Second City on Broadway. We swallowed hard, pretended to think it over, then agreed.

Of course our actors were delighted. All of us were swept up in this great adventure. Our dreams were about to come true—but I quickly had a rude awakening. One of the most gratifying aspects of my new life was the camaraderie I perceived between every person involved with The Second City. Here was a nearly ideal community based on trust. So I thought. When we announced the Broadway venture and offered contracts that were as generous as we could devise, the general euphoria among many of the actors turned to suspicion and paranoia. Were we deceiving them? What were we getting out of it? Now people whom I felt were my friends were sending their lawyers to make sure they were not being cheated. I had to accept the fact that I was dealing with an organizational law: there is a divide, no matter how small, between producer and actor. This was difficult to accept but necessary. To this day, though most of the hundred or so actors who worked for me remain friends in many ways, there is always, except for a handful, that little separation of wariness. Producing is a separating function. To deny that is to court disappointment.

In July 1961 we replaced our company in Chicago with Del Close, Joan Rivers, Avery Schreiber, and Melinda Dillon. The Broadway cast was made up of Alan Arkin, Barbara Harris, Severn Darden, Mina Kolb, Eugene Troobnik, and Andrew Duncan. Bill Matthieu was our pianist. The plan was first to open the Broadway cast at the Ivar Theater in Hollywood, play there for the summer while polishing the show, and then take the seasoned show to Broadway.

We were amazed and amused at that Los Angeles opening. William Morris and the Ivar people had pushed the boat out: red carpet, klieg lights, minor celebrities, television cameras. To us it looked like the Academy Awards in miniature. On the pavement stood a small knot of autograph seekers, humble, egoless people diffidently proffering their little books for signatures to anyone who seemed important. As I was leaving the theatre with one of the actors, one of these "fans" actually asked me for my autograph, but only after, at his request, I was able to point out my name in the program.

I have never ceased to marvel at the awe with which many members of the general public approach actors—close to a religious veneration. For them the actors possess some mysterious, transforming power, perhaps because creating a role is like creating a person.

The sumptuous opening-night party, at a fashionable Hollywood restaurant, was paid for by William Morris. Cigars all around and more minor glitterati. Nothing but flattering words and rosy predictions, free-flowing wine, and food on pointy sticks. It was a long way from one-dollar bentwoods on Wells Street in Chicago. And it had been only eighteen months since our opening.

The Ivar engagement went well. Reviews were glowing, attendance was good enough to make the theatre owners happy. So, in September 1961 when we opened at the Royale Theater, we were pretty cocky about conquering Broadway.

Broadway! It certainly was seductive. We who had swept out our own theatre, made our own schedules, turned out our own lights after replacing the bulbs, now had minions at our bidding, minions who were insulted if not allowed to serve our every whim and who, if we were at a loss for whims, would invent some whims for us.

We had status, standing, and recognition. We were special. The streets of New York, the very buildings cried out to us, "Success. Success. Success." We succumbed, all of us. The degree of enthrallment varied, but we all yielded. Never mind that we were living in a fleabag of a hotel on Forty-seventh Street called, if I remember correctly, the Piccadilly. If you cleared a spot on the dirty window you could make out there, across the street, on the marquee of the Royale Theater, the title of our show, "From The Second City."

Now, mark this: we had moved a show, basically intact, from our one-hundred-twenty-seat theatre in Chicago, where the admission price was two dollars and fifty cents, to the thousand-seat house in New York, where the admission price was twenty-some dollars. We still had no set, just our bentwoods. For costumes we brought our motley collection of jackets and our spectacles without lenses. We didn't use a curtain. The actors were paid a bit more, but not much more. Of course we now had ten stagehands, most of whose time was spent, as far as I could see, in betting on the show's chances for longevity: slim to none were, I think, the two choices. Oh yes, and there were three unused union musicians on the payroll (aptly called "walkers").* Also a union house manager, union company manager, union press agent, shamelessly high advertising costs, huge theatre rentals, and on and on. Since there were few changes in the show itself between Wells Street and Broadway, the cost differences could be almost entirely attributed to the delivery system— a sad situation that still prevails today. On Broadway the art continues to be relatively cheap, but the delivery is dear.

---

*The story goes that our friend David Merrick, understandably chafing at the idea of paying musicians for whom he had no need, installed them with their instruments to play in the theatre's "Gentlemen's Lounge."

In our case we were clearly hurt by the system. We had good to mixed reviews in the papers. People in "the business" were highly complimentary (Richard Rodgers wrote us a wonderful letter headed "Dear Second Citizens," in which he praised every aspect of our show), but we were consistently falling short of our twenty-thousand-dollar-a-week break-even point by a thousand or two. After two months we closed, honorably but inevitably.

We and the cast had lost a little of our innocence. For those of us who went back to Chicago, it was mostly innocence regained—though, like lost virginity, one cannot completely regain it. When I sobered up, it turned out to be a great lesson for me. I looked back and felt some shame at falling for the seduction of it all. I was grateful that we had Chicago to fall back on. From then on, I vowed, we would take care of our base, Chicago, first. Everything else, including New York and London and Hollywood, was to be considered, at least by me, as "the road." The rest of the world was interesting, possibly profitable, never home.

For the actors, who of course dreamed of thespian glory, it was a greater blow. And, sadly, it was the starting point of Paul Sills's departure, first from Chicago and then from The Second City.

Yes, we were a flop by Broadway standards. It was an honorable try and often well received but nevertheless a flop because the backers lost their investment. But we did create New York fans, including two nonshowbiz New Yorkers named Charley Rubin and Murray Zweig. Charley owned a number of coffee shops, most of them heavily mortgaged, and Murray was an accountant. Those two decided they wanted to be in show business, and we were to be their entrée.

Charley and Murray were typical New York mixtures of sophistication and provincialism, realism and fantasy, good humor and dark moods, that made them easy to talk with and hard to explain things to. Through thick and thin, we all remained fond of them. They took us on an inspection tour of Fourth Street, just off Broadway, to a large nightclub, then empty. At the time it was called Square East; it is now known as The Bottom Line. It was a good space. "This can all be ours," said Charley and Murray.

We committed to the two neophytes. We had no trouble convincing the actors to stay in New York. In fact we would have had a great deal of trouble convincing them to return to Chicago. And so our company moved from upper Broadway to lower Broadway. Although such an immediate move was against Equity rules, we appealed and won an exception. By November 1961 we were installed in Square East, where we survived for three turbulent years. (Attendance was boosted enormously by an appearance on David Susskind's TV show.)

Not long after we opened at Square East we were the subject of the first of many talent raids. Barbara Harris was offered the lead in a play called *Oh Dad, Poor Dad, They've Hung You in the Closet and You're Feeling So Sad.* Then Alan Arkin was offered a Broadway role. For the rest of our Square East run, the attrition rate among our actors was a constant problem. Here they were, working actors in a world where most actors were out of work, and they were sought out by agents who promised them the moon. True, we had them under contract, but none of us felt the slightest inclination to stand in their way if they had an important offer. In the New York world of show business, as an actor your career and its progress are in the forefront of your mind. The work at hand is often less important in itself than as a stepping-stone to fame and fortune. So it was, inevitably, with our cast. This drive to success is almost irresistible, and it is pervasive throughout our community. Nor were we Second City social critics immune to it. Those of the cast who hadn't yet achieved fame and fortune were surely trying for it, and who could blame them? All of this was accentuated by the New York buzz about our talent that quickly spread. Producers and casting agents were thick on the ground. Our replacement rate was nearly unsupportable. (I remember—it might have been sometime in 1964—Paul and I walking down Broadway on a matinee day and visiting backstage with three of our actors in three different shows.)

It was then that I began to appreciate an aspect of the Chicago theatre scene that had never occurred to me before. In New York or California, in the centers of "show business," if one does get a chance to work it's a high-stake and often one-shot venture. Strike out and there is seldom a second chance. In Chicago, we in the theatre are granted a magnificent right not accorded our coastal colleagues: the right to fail. Here an actor or director or playwright can present the work without paying the price of oblivion for not succeeding. Here one can try, fail, pick oneself up, and try again with little penalty. And while in Chicago ambition is always there, it can be safely stowed in the margins of your mind. It does not inform the work on a minute-to-minute basis. And there is no "scene" in Chicago, no big TV series around the corner, no Broadway stage, no movie industry. So the work can be done for its own sake rather than for where it might get you. This means better work.

Robert Klein (left) and Fred Willard in one of their wurst scenes. This was done for a television pilot that never made it to the air—and it's easy to see why.

I can remember that in the early days of the Steppenwolf Theatre, they mounted a wonderful production of *Balm in Gilead*, directed by John Malkovich, with Gary Sinise, Jeff Perry, Laurie Metcalf, and the entire Steppenwolf ensemble. From Chicago they took it to an Off-Broadway theatre. But because the cast was so large, they could take only some of the original company. So they recast about half of it with New York actors. My wife and I went to New York to see that production, and it was almost ludicrous. The Steppenwolf actors were playing ensemble. They were giving and unselfish, serving the play, while the New York actors, no matter how small their roles, were broadly emoting, each in his or her isolated space, as if the entire audience were composed of casting directors there to be impressed. It didn't require a great deal of sensitivity to identify which actors were from Chicago and which from New York.

Yes, after our New York experience Chicago was safe, Chicago was nurturing. All was fine, except for one problem. I returned from the Broadway wars to find a great deal of uneasiness around the theatre. Paul Sills was remaining in New York in what was a more or less permanent move. Cassandras were everywhere. Our demise was widely expected, even by the Chicago cast. After all, Paul had been the artistic mainspring of The Second City venture, and now, clearly, his sights were set elsewhere. What's more, our original cast was gone. From the start the experts had confidently predicted we wouldn't last a year. We were well past that, but who would take bets on our survival now?*

It took us a while to still our feelings of panic and desertion. Skeptics abounded, even in our own theatre—especially in our own theatre. It would have been easy to call it an honorable day. Why I didn't, I don't know. Stubbornness? Pride?

---

*Paul stayed in New York, directing at Square East and returning to Chicago two or three times to direct a show for us. He had a success on Broadway with his Story Theatre version of Ovid's *Metamorphosis*, later a TV series, and moved to Wisconsin, where he mounts shows and occasionally journeys to New York and elsewhere to teach. His contributions to the theatre with The Second City and Story Theatre, as well as with his teaching to a whole generation of actors, have been enduring.

I appointed Sheldon Patinkin as our director; Del Close returned to our stage as an actor; and we carried on. More realistically, we *held* on. No one, myself included, would confidently predict our survival.

3
The Sixties: London

In 1961, just after our Broadway opening, we moved our Chicago home to a new space we had built (financed by outside investors) next door to the old Chinese laundry. We had enough extra land to build an outdoor beer garden, where we showed our small collection of old films over and over on a large screen. (I can still describe every frame of Buster Keaton's *The General*.) Again Jimmy Masucci, who had designed the first Second City, worked his magic. He salvaged some ordinary boards about to be burned in a nearby incinerator. By adroit placement he created a stately wall for the beer garden, a wall that provided effective refuge from the street and, incidentally, for those wounded by the police in the riots at the 1968 Democratic convention.

All through the sixties, in fact until the mid-seventies, despite our low operating costs we were in poor economic shape. We overspent. We were wasteful. But each day I looked around and marked the fact that we were still alive. Considering our prospects at the beginning, every day was a gift.

So what the hell! Sheldon was directing. Joyce was producing. And by the end of 1963 I was London bound for a long stay.

Even as America in the early sixties was shaking off the weight of McCarthyism and of blind materialism, staid old England was transforming itself. In Liverpool four young men calling themselves the Beatles were making a splash. In the capital itself Mary Quant was pushing the fashion world into a marvelous eccentricity. A shabby little thoroughfare just off Piccadilly Circus, a street called Carnaby, was turning into a teeming marketplace, part carnival, all camp.

After the unspeakably dreary postwar years, the merry was returning to merry old England. The Kings Road swarmed with young people sporting rainbow-colored Mohawks and with skinheads, their anatomies pierced in various places with safety pins. Intelligent, talented young rebels spawned at Oxford and Cambridge—people like Peter Cook, Dudley Moore, Alan Bennett, and Jonathan Miller—were entering the show business stream. They were irreverent, highly verbal, mocking, and clever—the generation whose fathers had defeated Hitler. They mounted a wonderful review called "Beyond the Fringe"; founded *Private Eye*, a magazine devoted to exposing the chicanery of the establishment (published to this day); and, down on Greek Street in Soho, opened their equivalent of The Second City and defiantly called it the Establishment.

In October 1962 we traded companies with the Establishment for a limited run. Both the Establishment actors and their audiences were far raunchier than we were. Even our company rebel, Del Close, whom nothing ever fazed, was a bit taken aback on our opening night at the Establishment. On asking for an activity to serve as the subject matter for an improvised scene, the least of the rude offerings called out was "Fucking a duck."*

In turn, the Establishment company playing in Chicago managed to offend some Midwest sensibilities, first with an impious scene whose main characters were a hippy Jesus on the cross and the thieves who shared his fate; then with a short scene in which an unwanted pregnancy was terminated by the boyfriend sticking a pin in the balloon-enhanced stomach of one of the British actresses.

Some years later, when Monty Python was making a splash, I was asked what distinguished that group from The Second City. The rough answer—and it applied to the Establishment as well—is that we tended toward the humor of behavior and they emphasized the humor of comment. At our best we included ourselves as the subject of ironic criticism, and at their best they brilliantly sent up the establishment. Neither was better, just different. In fact, reading a Second City scene often leads to head-scratching. There are no obvious jokes. It doesn't seem all that funny. Because it is so behavior based, the comedy of our scenes comes not from how the words read on the page but how they play on the stage.

Just before I agreed to the trade with the Establishment, I had been talking to a young TV director at our local ABC station. His name was William Friedkin. He was an intense young man, so intense, talented, and obsessed with film that I was not surprised when he later won an Oscar for *The*

---

*For years after our opening we did not curse on stage, not out of principle or prudery but because it never occurred to us that these words might belong in our scenes. Now, as in so much of our culture, expletives are used with such frequency in film, on TV, and even on The Second City stage that they've lost their currency.

French Connection and startled filmgoers with *The Exorcist.* He loved The Second City and was itching to put us on film.

This was a time in the history of television when even the local stations made documentaries. The two of us talked with the adventurous general manager of our local ABC station, a dear man named Red Quinlan. He okayed a half-hour show about the trade between The Second City and the Establishment. Being part of that show was my first extensive experience in television. We filmed interviews with the casts, arrivals in London and Chicago, opening nights in both cities. Friedkin was in his element. The man never stopped moving, never slept. He was a demon behind the camera, a demon in the editing room. He wore me out. I often wondered whether it was something he ate. The program, titled "Tale of Two Cities," aired some days after our openings.

Despite the differences in approach, the London trade was a great success. The Establishment company, before returning home, went on to play Washington, D.C., and New York City. As to our cast, after ingesting the heady London atmosphere (most of them had never been abroad; in London they were housed in snooty Eaton Square, made much of by the press, and all in all came away thinking this was the way life should be lived), they reluctantly returned to the Chicago stage.

In our next London appearance we were the unwitting ploys in a high-stakes game. In the summer of 1963 I had a call from a Harold Fielding. In a high-pitched voice with a nonestablishment accent, he made it clear that he would like to produce us at his newly acquired theatre, the Prince Charles, just off Leicester Square. What I didn't know at the time was that Fielding had bought the property, a small legitimate theatre, with the intention of turning it into a cinema, only to be barred by the local council from making the change. His petition maintained that the Prince Charles, in size and configuration, was economically unsuitable for modern legitimate theatre use, but the council didn't buy it. His interest in our success was, to say the least, ambiguous.

We opened at the Prince Charles in the early fall, with a pickup cast in a review called "Looking for the Action."* Although we were praised extravagantly by some of the press and respectfully considered by others, we managed to prove Fielding's thesis in a couple of weeks. We later received the *Evening Standard* award for "Best Review of 1963," but we closed rather quickly. Some of the cast darkly hinted that we had been sabotaged, that the PR effort on our behalf was less than enthusiastic, but there was no proof. Nevertheless, armed with our failure, Fielding renewed his petition. This time it was granted and lo! to this day the Prince Charles is a movie house.

Unsuccessful as the Prince Charles engagement was, it did lead to a rather momentous set of events for me, both artistic and personal. The program people at Granada Television, an independent company located in Manchester, had been following our London engagements with great interest. They called and asked if I would be interested in doing a

*This title was taken from the scene that occupied the entire second act. It was the longest piece we had ever done, and it came very near to working as a longer form. It dealt with two conventioneers who, when telling their taxi driver they are "looking for the action," are driven to a strange house where they go through a series of real-life experiences, including acting as a judge in a death-penalty case and participating in the Bay of Pigs invasion. Complete with visuals, it was a highly interesting attempt and remains to be further explored.

series of programs for them. I don't think they suspected how little I knew about television. I suggested a series of parody documentaries. "Why not?" they said.

In November 1963 I set out for Manchester, England, as the executive producer of six TV specials called "Second City Reports." Except for the little I'd learned in my brief experience with Friedkin, I had barely been inside a television studio, could just manage to tell a camera from a boom, didn't know the lingo, didn't understand the limits. In fact I was a television ignoramus. Executive producer, indeed.

In the weeks leading up to my trip I had been in mail contact with Jane Nicholl, a Granada employee who had been assigned as my associate producer. From the formal, businesslike tone of her letters, I had pictured a rather prim, perhaps even severe older woman with hair in a bun and glasses on a string. The reality was a dishy, black-booted, high-energy beauty who combined immense feminine appeal with an awesome knowledge of television production. Granada, as a company, was only seven years old, and Ms. Nicholl had started near its beginning, progressing through every department, learning on the way.* She mentored my executive producership, turning me from a complete novice into a fairly knowledgeable beginner, and taught me to pronounce schedule as shedule and spell program as programme. We married in 1969.

Manchester has gone through a mild renaissance in the

---

*In 1967 Jane went to work for CBS News in New York as a producer first for "CBS Reports," then for a new documentary show called "Sixty Minutes." She was one of a handful of women who achieved that status at that time in the field of documentaries.

last fifteen years, with its appearance and its amenities some-what improved. In the early sixties it was a cold and dismal city, a wasteland strewn with the grim buildings and dull vistas left behind by the early industrial revolution. But not far away is the Lake Country and the Yorkshire Moors and romantic Shropshire.

Professionally, the entire Granada experience for me was like a dream. Here was a group that, though commercial, had more than the bottom line as their goal. They appreci-ated and encouraged quality work. Although they were com-peting with other independent television companies for airtime, their values were the equivalent of ours at The Sec-ond City. The Granada people, from Sidney Bernstein, head of the company (later Lord Bernstein), to Denis Forman, pro-gram, excuse me, programme director (later Sir Denis For-man), to Jane Nicholl (later Jane Nicholl Sahlins) to all the staff, were helpful, able, kind and enthusiastic, bright and sensitive.

Compared to the bottom-liners who rule American com-mercial media, Granada people qualified for canonization in TV heaven. They recruited from the universities and the in-tellectual media. For example, Derek Granger, hired just before I came on, who soon produced the incredible "Brideshead Revisited" series, had been a serious drama critic for a leading London paper with no television experi-ence whatsoever. But Denis Forman carefully brought him along, as he did the annual crop of college graduates he as-siduously recruited. Plunging into that atmosphere was ex-hilarating. Sadly those old standards no longer apply to English television, even to the BBC.

I hired as actors and writers John Bird, John Fortune, Eleanor Bron, and others of the Establishment people who had appeared in Chicago, so it was like being with old friends.*

The shows went well, and I returned four months later, but to a much-changed Second City scene. While I had been in England, John Kennedy had been assassinated, and in the winter of 1964 we were a saddened cast in a saddened country. Joyce and Sheldon had been holding the fort in Chicago, but the appetite for topical comedy during a protracted mourning period was diminished. Our money problems continued. New York's Square East closed in November 1964. I managed to borrow ten thousand dollars to keep us afloat, but for a year or two it was touch and go. The mood of the country was restless and hedonistic, and so was the mood of our casts. The big talents on which we had founded the theatre were gone. Now it was as though we were starting over.

Watching our first company leave one by one was painful. Despite the necessary distance between management and actor, it always hurt to see someone leave. To this day Second City actors, what with classes, touring companies, and the main stage, are around for at least two years and many of them for longer. When they leave, it is a little like losing a loved one. Their unique qualities are, one feels, irreplaceable. And we are used to their strengths and weaknesses, emphasizing the one and covering for the other. I don't think I fired more than two or three actors in twenty-five years.

*One of the new writers I hired had impressed me with his humorous newspaper columns for the *Guardian*. Although he hadn't worked in television, his graceful wit made me laugh out loud. His name was Michael Frayn, now highly regarded as a playwright and novelist (*Copenhagen*, *Noises Off*, and others). We joke to this day about how I launched his career.

Not that there weren't worthy replacements for that first company. David Steinberg, Burns and Schreiber, Fred Willard, Robert Klein, Peter Boyle—all came on in the sixties, but they came on as journeymen actors, and without the University of Chicago connections and shared theatre links that we had all had with one another. Musical genius Bill Matthieu left in 1964 to be replaced by musical genius Fred Kaz, master of the musical pun. (If an improvised scene dealt with babies, for example, and if one listened closely, the unobtrusive underscoring would be a minor-key "Yes, sir, that's my baby," or "Babes in arms," or "My baby don't care for me.")

A bright spot was the fact that we were able to continue working with Friedkin. The two of us managed to convince Red Quinlan to do a couple of parody documentaries, one of which nearly led to dire consequences. The idea was to do a send-up of commercial holidays called "Love in America Day." Friedkin managed to enlist the entire resources of a small, and, as it turned out, redneck town some sixty miles south of Chicago. Under the impression this was a serious event, they turned out the high school marching band, the American legion's floats, the Shriners, the Kiwanis, and extensive police escorts. The mayor and other city officials were installed on a rostrum along Main Street, and the entire town served as extras on the parade route.

But, as I say, it was a send-up. Our actors on the floats were dressed up as George and Martha Washington, Romeo and Juliet, Heloise and Abelard, all kissing on signals. We had black people, of whom the town had none, playing roles. About halfway through the parade, the locals started to sense that we were making fun of George Washington, the town, and the subject matter in general. Things started to get ugly.

We quickly assembled and rode out of town before they could effectively marshal their forces, but it was a near thing. I can still see Avery Schreiber, who played George Washington, riding shotgun in a convertible, his white wig flapping in the breeze as we hightailed it down Route 66. The program turned out well, but even today there is a little corner of Illinois where we do not go.

This period also saw the start of our touring company. By 1967 the requests for one- to two-night appearances at colleges were mushrooming. I wasn't particularly keen on diverting energy and resources to another company, but the training aspect of the venture, the fact that we could, in effect, field a farm team, ready to feed our main stage, won me over. Now The Second City keeps three touring companies busy, with staff dedicated to managing them all. Then we had Joyce Sloane, alone, to book, arrange transport and accommodations, and take care of the paperwork.

What I hadn't realized was that in creating a touring company we had arranged a useful sort of purgatory (the actors called it Touring Company Hell) to which we could send main-stage people who were screwing up. I believe we sent George Wendt, of "Cheers" fame, to Hell twice before he became a stable fixture of the regular company.

In 1967 we said goodbye to Masucci's phone-booth walls and stately beer garden to move two blocks down the street. Here, in what is still The Second City's Chicago location, we seated more than three hundred.

We saved and transported one relic. In 1961, when we were building our second theatre, heedless developers were tearing down the Garrick Theater, a remarkable Louis Sullivan building in the Loop. Preservation is still an uphill battle, but the idea had even fewer adherents then. Just as the wrecking ball (we named our first show in the new space "The Wrecking Ball") was smashing into the Garrick, I managed, for the princely sum of fifteen hundred dollars, to rescue four decorated ten-foot columns surmounted by a relief containing four sculpted heads of classical musicians. (The Garrick had originally served as an opera house.) The columns and heads served as our entryway, and because I was able to move them once more, they remain as The Second City's entrance.

4
The Next Generation

Toward the end of the sixties I sensed we were in the midst of a fallow period. The cast, while talented and funny, had no intellectual background, the ironic spark that I was looking for. Audiences reacted well, but the edge was missing. The cast was too old. They were performers, not actors. Their material veered from the worthy. They had rough personalities.

On the other hand, in the touring company was a group that really intrigued me. They were young and exceptionally bright, educated, with a high reference level. They reminded me of our first cast, but they were distinctly of their own time—Harold Ramis, Brian Doyle Murray, Jim Fischer, Judy Morgan, Roberta Maguire, David Blum. I was attracted by their enthusiasm, their work ethic, and the freshness of their outlook. They and their stage manager, an aspiring young actor named Joe Flaherty, often called rehearsals on their own just to develop material. And they were generous with one another.

From left, David Blum, Harold Ramis, Roberta Maguire, and Joe Flaherty. Despite rumors to the contrary, real marijuana was not used in this scene about getting stoned.

I wanted to work with these bright, energetic actors on the main stage. Problem: how to deal with the incumbents. In an intervention just short of divine, we received an offer to appear in New York at a theatre on East Sixty-fourth Street. Naturally the resident cast was delighted. What actor would not want to appear in New York—though of course they would have to be replaced in Chicago.

I deny, deny, deny—as some maintained at the time and still do—that this New York episode was an elaborate ploy on my part to rid ourselves of an old cast in order to install a new one. For one thing, the New York invitation came from out of the blue, unsolicited. And I made it clear to those who wanted to fill the engagement that there was an excellent chance they might not be coming back. That gave none of them a moment's pause. They were raring to go. Nothing unusual about that. Show me the actor who, given the chance to showcase in New York, does not expect that the divine hand of fame will point her beckoning finger at him.

We did not fare especially well in that New York engagement, but I did have my new cast in place in Chicago, with however, no director in sight. Since 1963 Sheldon Patinkin had directed many of the shows in Chicago and even the closing show at Square East. All this time his interest in music had continued. A chance to work with Leonard Bernstein on *Candide* was something he couldn't turn down. In 1968 he left The Second City and Chicago and moved to New York. He returned from time to time, helping me with our television show in Toronto and directing some shows there, but he moved on to the chairmanship of the Theater and Music Department of Columbia College in Chicago, remaining with The Second City as a consultant.

Directors for our kind of work were—and remain—thin on the ground. In addition to all the usual requirements of staging, helping actors, and mediating egos, a Second City director, because he is involved in developing material, also acts as a head writer and an editor. Add to that a skill at devising running orders and a talent for dealing with musical issues. Where does the training come from for such a role? Through the years we had tried outside directors with middling to poor results. Now we had an eager young cast especially in need of guidance, and no director in sight.

I had never much wanted to direct. I still didn't, but what the hell! I really liked our new group. In effect we were all starting from scratch. I decided to try it. We started rehearsals.

Just before the first meeting, I was approached by the cast en masse. Would I consider moving Joe Flaherty out of his stage manager role and making him a cast member? I agreed for political reasons and quickly came to rejoice for artistic ones. Joe was and is one of the best actors and improvisers we ever had.

Rehearsals went smoothly. The differences between the new cast and the old were striking. Ramis and company thought of themselves as beatniks (a misinterpretation of the sixties rebellion). True they had long hair and liked to deny received wisdom. Their musical tastes had been nurtured on doo-wop and had matured to rock and roll, but unlike the real beatniks, there was a sweetness behind their protest, and they had an advanced talent for self-irony and a fundamental respect for civility. Actually they were the successors to the rebellious sixties—mature, less alienated, middle class. The insurgency of the sixties was now victorious and these, its heirs, had incorporated it and moved on. Listening to them, I was learning a lot about what this post-sixties generation was thinking.

Although I didn't mark it at the time, this was the youngest cast we'd had to date. The first cast had been theatre veterans, some of them really old—in their thirties! Subsequent casts were similarly composed. Now, most of the actors in this new company were in their early twenties. Their energy was phenomenal. They were just as inventive and intelligent and well read as our first cast, but they wore their culture differently. The intellectual took second place to their music, their politics, and their ways of living. They had this sweetness about them. They were more secure than their immediate forebears. And they could accept success, even middle-class success.

Early on as a director I learned an important lesson for review work. Listen to your cast. Don't impose your own attitudes toward drugs, toward sex, toward politics on them. If they are intelligent and educated, they will bring their own ironic light to bear on what interests them and their audiences, and it's going to be slightly different from yours. The actors and the audiences stay the same age (eighteen to thirty-five). Only the director gets older. In this work the job of the director is to hold to standards of intelligent discourse and skilled acting, not to dictate attitudes and content. By listening to his cast, the director in fact finds out what's going on in their world. What struck me in the process is how attitudes change, ever so slightly but perceptibly, in a school generation of about four years. This manifested itself vividly in comparing actors from our different companies who were brothers: the Belushis, the Murrays (there were three of them: Brian Doyle, Bill, and Joel), the Flahertys. The slight differences in their values and preoccupations weren't due to sibling positioning vis-à-vis each other but represented a small turn of time's wheel.

It turned out that this was indeed a new generation as well as a turning point—for them and for me. Except for Joyce, the old faces—Sheldon, Paul, Howard—were gone. For ten years I had been learning, building up steam, living the life of the theatre but never quite of it, deferring to those with more experience and confidence. Now, for the first time, I felt at home: sure of myself and in control.

It was a good time. I enjoyed it, they enjoyed it. They were quick to turn their ironic talents on themselves. We did a good show and it worked for the audiences. In a break from our usual practice of non sequitur show titles, we aptly called this one "The Next Generation." We knew this represented a watershed. There was a sense of rebirth and joy around the theatre. What I didn't realize at the time was that the character of this cast was a harbinger of a sea change in the culture of The Second City. The world was about to pour in on us and I, for one, with all my newfound confidence, wasn't ready for it. But first, I backtrack to 1963 and our foray into Canada.

5
The Invasion of Canada

"Canada? I don't even know what street it's on."—
Al Capone

By 1963 we had developed "alumni," a group of actors who had worked with us and on whom we could call for short engagements. Our Canadian connection started with such an engagement in the spring of that year with a week at the Royal Alex Theater in Toronto. Its improbable owner, who deserves to be on anybody's list of unforgettable characters, was an original named Ed Mirvish, who at this writing is going strong in partnership with his son David. A couple of years before our appearance at the Royal Alex, while the bluebloods of self-righteous Toronto society were helplessly wringing their hands, each looking at the next man to do something about the impending demise of this thousand-seat theatre, "this merchant" who knew nothing about the theatre business, stepped in and bought it, as he bought everything, for cash.

Ed Mirvish was no ordinary merchant. He was the most peculiar blend of shrewdness and innocence I have ever encountered. On the one hand he was obviously one of Canada's greatest business success stories, with a flair for the dramatic gesture. On the other hand, in social situations he was soft-spoken, considerate, unpretentious, and candid. He owned one of the world's first and largest discount houses, Honest Ed's Warehouse. Each day huge shipments of everything from radios to carpenter's nails, from clothing to garden hose, would pour into the Warehouse, with every single piece of every shipment placed on the floor. Aisles existed in name only. These wholesale lots were acquired at bargain prices by a brigade of buyers who rode through Canada and the upper United States in cars with the appellation HONEST ED'S BUYER prominently painted on the doors.*

With no prior theatrical experience, Ed Mirvish made the Royal Alex successful. He ran a season of musicals and then single-week attractions. We were one of the latter and we did well. At the end of the engagement we promised to return.

We did so the following year, and again the year after. They loved us in Canada. Nathan Cohen, the revered critic for the *Toronto Star,* wrote elegies about us. The CBC had us on television. We were courted. In 1973 we succumbed. With Toronto businessmen practically throwing checks at us, we agreed to open a permanent Second City in Toronto. Since the review form, as we established it, spoke to its own com-

---

*Ed's Warehouse fronted on a square-block area called Markham Square. When the residents of the square refused him permission for a parking lot, he bought every house in the square and not only built his parking lot but preserved most of the houses, which he rented out to restaurants, art galleries, and a bookstore.

munity, it was important that at least part of the cast be Canadian.

In the spring of 1973, Joyce Sloane and I went north on a casting expedition. Talent galore. Perhaps it is the position of Canada vis-à-vis the giant United States that accounts for an abundance of ironists, but they certainly proliferate there. From a local production of *Godspell* we chose Gilda Radner, Jerry Salzman, Jayne Eastwood, and later Eugene Levy. Two aspirants who had heard about our quest showed up at our hotel, followed us around, and generally dogged us to audition them. Their names were Dan Aykroyd and Valri Bromfield. They wore us out, and we finally acceded to their request. It took no more than ten minutes. Joyce and I looked at each other. "We've seen enough," I bellowed. They looked up, startled. "You're hired. Now get some better clothes." Later a lovely actress named Catherine O'Hara auditioned so well that our usual chauvinist lineup of four men and two women, was expanded on the female side.

From the United States I brought Brian Doyle Murray and Joe Flaherty. Rehearsals were a breeze. Mostly we played football in the empty lot near the storefront in the downtown area that we had rented as our theatre.

In rehearsal the Canadians vindicated our choices. They were far less interested in politics than we were and much closer to general show business, but they were funny, quirky, intelligent. They immediately bonded with the Yanks, and the show was seamless. All seemed to be going swimmingly for our scheduled opening at the beginning of September. Then, in the week before the first preview, things turned ominous.

First, our application for a liquor license was stalled. Toronto was a much more Puritan town in those days, and

John Candy, Dan Aykroyd, Eugene Levy, Rosemary
Radcliff, and Gilda Radner outside the doors of the
Toronto Second City. Long hair was in.

the liquor laws were even more stringent than were those dealing with adultery.

Second, we were experiencing the greatest late-summer heat wave in recorded history, and our theatre was not air-conditioned. Worse, most of the building was glass, so the temperature in the theatre room inside was a good ten degrees hotter than the official outside readings—which even at night were in the nineties. By the time things grew really worrisome, we had neither the money nor the time to install air-conditioning. Our only recourse was prayer; that and painting all the glass black and spraying it with water, which didn't help at all.

The heat lingered for weeks. The cast labored mightily, changing clothes frequently during the show. Reviews were positive. We would start each show with a full house, but because of the heat we would finish to empty seats, having given refunds to most of the audience. Of course the heat wave eventually broke, but we were done in by the continued absence of a liquor license. After six months we closed.

Our effort did not go unapplauded. An enterprising young man working in marketing for the O'Keefe Center, Toronto's mammoth downtown concert and theatre facility,* had fallen in love with the group. Andrew Alexander called me about continuing in a facility he could rent from the city. It was an attractive old fire hall, two streets from where we had flopped.

---

*Mike Nichols and Elaine May, in a two-person show produced by Alexander H. Cohen, were presented for preview performances at the O'Keefe Center, capacity of thousands. The show started with the tiny figure of Mike Nichols standing stage center. Cupping his hands to his mouth, he shouted at the top of his lungs to the cavernous house, "Alexander H. Cohen presents—an intimate Review-view-view-view."

Martin Short (left), Steven Kampmann, and Peter Torkvei in a scene at The Second City, Toronto. This was not standard stage dress.

"Yes," he assured me in answer to my question. "It is air-conditioned. Yes, I have a liquor license."

We agreed on terms that left the art to us, and in late 1974 we opened. Andrew is a first-class producer, and The Second City is still going strong in Toronto. Talent kept pouring out of this Canadian spigot. John Candy auditioned, and we were so impressed we sent him to fill a vacancy in the Chicago company. (John stayed with the Chicago company for six months, after which he was needed in Toronto. He was reluctant to go, and I had to assure and reassure him that this wasn't a demotion. He finally agreed that returning to Canada wasn't such a bad idea when he got a chance to star in the SCTV series.) Martin Short, then Dave Thomas later joined the company. I directed the first show, and this time everything was cool. It was an exhilarating time for me, like reliving the first days of The Second City in Chicago.

My Granada experience in television, besides getting me a wife, had left me with some residual knowledge of TV and a liking for the fact that it seemed to be a finite experience with a beginning, a middle, and an end.

In 1967, as an offshoot of our Royal Alex engagements, I had produced and written a TV program for the CBC about the rivalry between Montreal (then much the more dominant of the two cities) and Toronto, especially in hockey. The comic thesis of the show was that Montreal had developed an atom bomb and was threatening its use on Toronto should Montreal not win the Stanley Cup. That year we also appeared on the CBC in a segment of a terrific magazine show, a precursor of "Sixty Minutes" called "This Hour Has Seven Days."

Once we were permanently ensconced in Toronto, and with Harold Ramis as head writer, we mounted two half-hour variety shows for Canadian TV that we called, tongue in cheek, "Gangway for Comedy." They were flawed but with enough merit to serve as a calling card. Andrew Alexander and I met with a small five-station network called Global TV, and by late 1976, as executive producer, I had put together a group of actor-writer talents that ranked with any in TV history: Harold Ramis, John Candy, Dave Thomas, Andrea Martin, Catherine O'Hara, Joseph Flaherty, and later, Martin Short and Rick Moranis.

We decided to lampoon television itself and came up with the notion of a tiny TV station in a one-horse town that did its own newscasts and entertainment programming. It was called SCTV (Second City Television).

While we were shooting the first SCTV series in
Toronto, the two sirs, John Gielgud and Ralph
Richardson, were performing there on stage. To our
surprise they agreed to appear in a scene on our program.
Naturally we took a picture. Front, from left, Sir Ralph
Richardson, Dave Thomas, Sir John Gielgud. Rear,
Bernie Sahlins, John Candy, Sheldon Patinkin,
Joe Flaherty, Catherine O'Hara, Andrew Alexander,
Rosanne Ironstone, Milad Bessada.

The first show provided an example of Karl Marx's dic-
tum that history repeats itself, first as tragedy and then as
farce. This time it was first comedy, then farce. As I look
back on it, I wonder what the hell I was thinking about.

When Second City started, we worried about connecting the scenes in some way, and at the suggestion of Mike Nichols we junked that idea and just presented our disparate scenes. When we wrote the first SCTV show we had as one element all those TV parodies, and, as a second element through-line situations with continuing characters: Eugene Levy as a security guard, John Candy as a blustering, failed actor returning to his home stomping grounds, and so forth.

Sheldon Patinkin, whom I had brought up as associate producer, and I sat down to edit all this into a coherent half-hour, and we were stumped. Combination after combination fizzled. Then it struck me, "Sheldon," I said, "we are stupid. This is exactly the situation when we brought in Mike Nichols at the start of The Second City, and the solution is the same." We threw out the story lines, and the show worked beautifully. When the shows grew longer there were more story lines, but these were never paramount.

After the first thirty shows (the show continued the following season), I had had my fill of series television. As I said before, I'm a beginning, middle, and end guy. Eugene Levy sagely observed that "In a television series, after the first four or five shows you're no longer learning anything, you're just doing what you know, just working away, filling the time. If it didn't pay so well, creative people would not do extensive television series."

He was right. It began to blur: traveling to Canada, living in hotels, sitting in control rooms, staring at editing screens, filling the half-hours, dealing with dozens of egos (and this was a cast that was unusually amicable). It all became too much, and since I didn't need to do it, I quit. Andrew Alexander, who is less flappable than I, ably stepped in as executive producer and took the show very far indeed.

6
John Belushi, the Seventies, and the End of Innocence

Halcyon days, those early seventies. Business was good. Our young company was going from strength to strength. I didn't realize that time's wheel was turning and a different age was coming.

One afternoon early in the decade I wandered backstage in Chicago and overheard a member of the touring company on the telephone. I shamelessly listened in as she uttered the words "pilot season" and "residuals." I was astounded. A rank beginner and *she had an agent!* 1959 was never like that!

A Lithuanian actor once told me that unless it gets new blood, the creative life of a theatre is over in twenty years. In the beginning the brilliance and vision of its founders (plus a lot of luck and great actors) propel it to high achievement. But at the fifteen-year point, when those founders should give way to the next generation, they are reluctant to let go of the reins, and the theatre slides downhill over the next five years. Was this happening to us? After all, this was the fifteen-year point. And was I entering into old-fogyism, threatened by change and dwelling in the good old days?

Until then, despite our welcome to the world outside of Chicago, despite a measure of success and recognition internationally, I felt we had been able to insulate ourselves from corrupting commercial values. We had been able to retain—snobbishly, no doubt—a faint disdain for success, even our own. This disdain extended to commercial show business, to politicians in general, to the best-seller list, to the popular just because it was popular. Just because a book is on the best-seller list doesn't necessarily mean that it's bad, but we didn't quite believe that.

From our beginnings we had tiptoed the boundary line where the classical spirit ends and the realm of commercial, popular entertainment begins. I knew that the trick was not to stray into either region while incorporating the best of both. Thus we never really appealed to a mass audience. Since we held on to certain anti-establishment values while preserving a floor of intelligent discourse, our audiences were primarily college kids and the sympathetic elite.

Our founding ideas led us to beware of the dangers of success and to roar against any changes in outlook that success might bring. And until the seventies we were able to maintain our insulation from the popular culture, even when, as in New York and on television, we were a minor part of it.

Too, we were kept in line by our audiences. While they

didn't exactly constitute a cult, our activities never appealed to the great majority. We never had the wide-ranging allure of rock stars, for instance, or of popular films and TV shows. And because most of our audience and all of our actors were young, we were not looking for the latest, the trendy. We *were* the latest and the trendy, and we were content to be a minority force in the large scene.

But a significant social change was taking place in a way that I was just beginning to perceive. The bright energy of the cast of "The Next Generation" came at a price.

Through most of the sixties, the youth culture—of which we were but a small, specialized part—operated as a sub-culture. Young people sang songs to other young people, played the jukeboxes for each other in drive-ins, lived in their own world that was largely hidden and separate from the world of their parents. They were not the dominant culture. No, the dominant culture was composed of adults. It was presided over by the media, reflected in the subject matter and attitudes of television and movies. In the early sixties the official media still bought into the values and symbols of the fifties. Most working writers, actors, and producers were past their youth. Their target audience was certainly not the very young.

All this began to change by the late sixties. Campus protests, beginning in the early years of the decade, had a profound impact on the larger culture. Youth took over: "Saturday Night Live," *Rolling Stone* magazine, sex, drugs, rock and roll. Their songs moved out of the drive-ins and reached everywhere, even into geriatric centers. Their watchwords, their attitudes, their anti-war message, their love-ins, their Woodstock, their marijuana took center stage. "Never trust anyone over thirty."

In Hollywood the median age of studio executives plummeted. Television became sillier. *Time* magazine and similar media jumped on the youth-culture bandwagon and helped roll it along. They trumpeted the coming of this new day, even took charge of it. Suddenly the multinational corporations too switched gears, coopting the youth culture's watchwords and symbols to sell things. And, before we realized it, we were swept up in the rush to an adolescent world.

One positive result of the youth takeover was the reawakening of Chicago as a theatrical town. Young people (including a group that had gone to school with David Mamet) were forming theatres, renovating spaces. As Richard Christiansen, chief critic for the *Chicago Tribune*, later pointed out, it was the survival of The Second City that proved a local theatre could succeed. Modestly he neglected to note that his own encouragement of these theatres, along with that of the *Sun-Times'* Glenna Syse, who shared his sympathies and passions for the theatre, played no small part in the burgeoning theatre scene. Christiansen and Syse reviewed every theatre event, even the smallest: the storefronts, the sixty-seaters. They reviewed them in their major newspapers with all the respect and understanding and space they accorded Broadway shows. Their reviews and attitudes built audiences. They must be credited with a key role in the rebirth of the local theatre scene. (I named one of our shows "Glenna Loved It" and presented her with a T-shirt bearing that title. She loved it.)

Fledgling theatres did come to us for advice and encouragement. So barren had been the scene that many of the typical questions were "How do you run a box office?" "How do you keep books?" "Where do you advertise?" At this date in 2000 there are more than 150 active theatre companies in Chicago. For the first time in my memory, actors are moving here from the East and West Coasts because there is more work. It is a source of personal pride that we played some part in this.

But along with this positive development there were features of the youth resurgence that disturbed me. One was the direction of its humor, exemplified by "Saturday Night Live." It was grounded in a bad-boyism whose main goal was willy-nilly to send up one's elders: parents, politicians, all established authority. I didn't mind the send-ups; it was the willy-nilly that bothered me.

On our own stage we were successfully able to fight the tendency (or at least make fun of it). But a second and more pernicious threat came from the heightened attention we were now receiving. Like our touring-company member with an agent, our work attitudes were affected. Being courted by—indeed now being part of—the mainstream brought changes in the attitudes of our actors and eventually of our theatre. It was another end-of-innocence experience, like our New York foray, only this time it affected our home base.

This was not a decline of talent or intelligence in our casts, not a devaluing of the work itself. It was a slight change in the direction of our goals, a slight opening for commercial considerations, a slight recasting of the role of The Second City as a stepping-stone to commercial success.

In this new day an actor or director coming to work for The Second City was a bit more likely to think of it as a prelude to "making it." Now the connections to Hollywood and Broadway were a little more immediate. Now "doing the work for its own sake" was slightly tinged with "Where is this work taking me?" Success in show business, which had been a remote possibility safely stowed in the margins of our minds, moved distinctly to the forefront of every actor's thoughts. That this must affect his work was certain. Commercial show-biz success, once a distant goal for most of us, became an immediate possibility.

These slight changes add up and in turn influence the actor's approaches to the stage and the material, not its high standards—directors can see to that—but in subtle ways its directions and emphases. As one of our actors observed, "I finished my work at Second City and stepped out the door to find myself having to accept and adjust to all the people and things we made fun of."

So the rise of the youth culture and the importance of our contributions to it changed The Second City forever. The great maw of this youth culture opened to swallow us up. We were hot, and the actors were in demand—for television, for movies.

This societal change was just one of the factors affecting our work. The other was cultural. At the beginning we had come from the theatre. Acting standards, references, structures, everything the work meant to us was derived from the stage. But the new generation was coming from television. References and attitudes and structures encased in some of our earlier work disappeared and still are gone. They have been replaced by other references, other attitudes. (It is a testimony to the flexibility of the review form that it can accommodate even the most dramatic changes in attitudes and perceptions.) Whether this change was positive, negative, or neutral is moot. But the touring-company actor on the telephone with her agent jolted me into an awareness that these changes were happening, that given the cultural climate they were inevitable, and that there wasn't anything I could do about it.

It was a tough realization for me. Clearly, if it is to survive, a theatre like The Second City must change over time. So long as that change is confined to attitudes, it is relatively easy to accept. Where values and goals are involved, acceptance is more difficult.

Part of the duties of a founder is to know when to give way to the new and not to characterize it as regressive. We should enjoy the deliciousness of the irony turned against us ironists. We should accept that our response to what was current carries the seeds of change that might displease us— or be beyond our understanding. We should rejoice at one more proof that our chosen form is so flexible as to accommodate these changes. We should, but it's hard.

The arrival on the scene of John Belushi accelerated this sea change at The Second City. Joyce Sloane and I were holding auditions in the early seventies when the regular company was being sent to appear at the Plaza Hotel in New York for a limited engagement. The touring company was appearing on our main stage, and we were hiring replacements for it. Joyce and I would approach auditions with weary dread laced with eternal hope.

This time, out on stage walked three students from a suburban college who had been bugging Joyce for an opportunity to show their stuff—scenes they had developed under the influence of The Second City. One of them was not tall, not handsome, not prepossessing, but unforgettable. Once he walked on stage, neither of us could take our eyes off him. His name was John Belushi. Not only did we hire him on the spot, but when the company returned we kept him on as a regular. His two companions, Tino Insana and Dick Blasucci, eventually came to work at The Second City. But it took no special eye for talent to see that Belushi had a rare power and presence to which no audience was immune.

It was inevitable that Belushi's talent would be quickly noticed on a national scale. By the time he hit our stage, we were a regular stopping-off point for television and movie people from both coasts searching for the next star. We thought of them as brigands, cruising in our waters, raiding our little ship for talent. We were fast becoming an unwilling talent pool for producers to fish in. Both *National Lampoon*, which at that time had a radio show, and later the NBC variety show "Saturday Night Live," were after Belushi from the moment they saw him. And no wonder. He commanded the stage. They were after Bill Murray too, and Harold Ramis and others.

Aside from his theatrical appeal, Belushi was a lodestar for his generation, the rebels after the cause of the Vietnam War. Sex, drugs, and rock and roll were his meat. But with all his excesses, his restlessness, his drive, there was a sweetness and even an innocence to Belushi. My fondest memory of him was invoked at his funeral by Harold Ramis. For one of our shows we had worked out a Bible scene that involved John coming on, after the opening, as an angel. He appeared at the upstage door with a pair of plastic wings poorly attached to his back. With those wings frantically flapping, he swooped downstage, crossing to comfort the Virgin Mary. For anyone else it would have been a ludicrously ungainly motion. But Belushi managed somehow, by the fetching awkwardness of his movement and indeed by his tenderness, to transform that simple stage cross into a moment so touching and—dare I say it—so sweet that a smile

John Belushi haranguing the establishment in a pro-crime rebuttal to a television editorial. "After all, criminals are responsible for the gainful employment of large numbers of policemen."

of delight brushed the face of everyone lucky enough to see it. In that moment he was, as Harold said, indeed an angel.

The ascent of Belushi, and of Gilda Radner, Bill Murray, Harold Ramis, John Candy, Dan Aykroyd, and the SCTV cast, but especially of Belushi, was the catalyst that sped the transformation of The Second City for good and bad from a Chicago theatre to a national institution. Now, if you were in Chicago for a convention or a holiday, you went to The Second City. Now, if you were a producer or a director or a casting agent, you came to The Second City on a talent hunt. Now, alongside the Symphony, the Lyric Opera, the museums, and the sports teams, The Second City was listed as a must-see Chicago attraction: the best of times, the worst of times.

Amidst this success, and for reasons easily recognized by resident directors, doing show after show was growing wearisome for me. I began to understand why Paul Sills had been so restless.

Proper directing has a down side that has to do with ego distribution. To risk a generalization that could get me lynched, actors—many actors—need a lot of attention. And their needs vary. Some require constant praise, some ask for minute specific directions, others prefer to explore. Good directors subdue their own ego needs in favor of the actor's, and that often leads to fruitful discoveries. The bad director is a tsar who imposes his vision. His discoveries were made by himself in advance.

My problem with trying to be a good director is exhaustion. I just don't have a large enough ego of my own continually to distribute pieces of it to others.

I had tried out a couple of outside directors, but the results were not good. Then Del Close called. He had been through the Haight-Ashbury scene in San Francisco, dried out at an alcohol aversion clinic in Texas, narrowed his drug habits to a couple of substances, and remained through it all a brilliant, funny, inspiring artist. I took a chance, and for a couple of years in the mid-seventies we were in turn inspired and maddened by Del Close. Casts loved him. He brilliantly personified the rebel, the ironist, the satirist.

Astonishing scenes were conceived under his direction, and there was great camaraderie between Del and the male

Tino Insana (left) and Bill Murray, when Hare Krishnas were allowed to solicit at airports.

cast members. Women were not as taken with him, nor he with them.* And there was one other problem: he was seldom a finisher. Basic ideas: brilliant. Nitty gritty of the scenes: not so brilliant. In a quite happy tandem, Del would do the brilliant work and I the journeyman's job, the cleaning up and ordering of the scenes to make a show. It was effective while it lasted. Eventually, by the end of the sev-

---

*Meagen Fay tells me that the only direction she ever got from Del Close was, "Why don't you paint your nipples green?"

enties, Del's excesses proliferated, and we were forced to part. He went on to become the legendary guru of pure improvisation, inspiring the formation of dozens of improv companies.

Back in the director's harness for the next few years, I worked with excellent casts. Now it's true that The Second City has a reputation for developing great comedy actors. But only part of the credit should go to our eye for talent. When one thinks about it, where in America does an actor train for comedy? Most Second City actors, between touring companies and the main stage, are around for three or four years. They play eight shows a week, "write" their own material, interact as ensemble members. After three or four years of that they stand a good chance of learning their craft.* They learn another thing too: that their stage life is in the hands of the actor playing opposite them. If he or she looks good, you look good. It's something many actors don't realize and will never learn.

For the rest of the seventies and the early eighties we had a run of excellent casts and solid shows. As has always been true, many of them went on to strong careers in the business. The Toronto Second City was also flourishing. I traveled there once or twice to direct a show and found fewer regional distinctions.

In 1984 I made our last foray into New York. The storied Village Gate (storied for the talent it presented, not for the comfort of its facilities) invited us to bring our current

---

*A Hollywood director once observed to me, "I can always tell when an actor has worked at The Second City. First of all, he's read the whole script, not just his own parts. Second, he creates a company feeling, so that whoever is playing opposite has a ground of solid, ensemble support."

Chicago show, "Orwell That Ends Well," for an open-ended engagement. Once again, as in most legitimate theatre ventures except for Toronto, we were marginally successful: not doing so badly as to close immediately, not doing so well as to extend for a long run. This time in New York I felt none of the seduction, none of the attraction of our previous visits. The cast, which included future television celebrities Richard Kind and Isabella Hoffman, was frantic for the show to continue, rightly viewing it as an important career move. I found myself curiously disinterested. For the first time in twenty-four years, I had a job and not a vocation.

Starting with the Village Gate engagement, a number of factors contributed to a lessening of my excitement. For one, I found fewer and fewer people to talk with. The passing of time had left me with less in common with the actors. Then too, with every new scene I found myself recalling an analogous old one. I couldn't bear being a bore. In fact I was boring myself. And, oh yes, Andrew Alexander made me an excellent offer.

In March 1985 I sold my interest in The Second City to Andrew. I had exceeded by five my stay of twenty years as prescribed by the Lithuanian actor. I remained as artistic director for a year, then left to work on many other things, all theatre related.

The Second City continues to flourish. The casts are skilled and intelligent. The material is worthy and well paced. A time traveler present in 1959 and again in 1999 would find many similarities, formal and in content. Our traveler would also notice important differences: fewer behavior scenes, a more presentational approach to the work, a greater separation between the characters played and the players. A shockproof cast playing to a shockproof audience.

But those audiences remain young and enthusiastic. Evidently The Second City is still providing what the times call for, and the virtues are certainly there. I must say, I enjoy the shows very much now. The elements I miss are compensated for by the innovative skills of the performers. I realize that those missing elements are important just to me. Perhaps that wheel will turn again. Perhaps not.

On December 16, 1999, The Second City celebrated its fortieth year. Among the festivities was a luncheon given for Joyce Sloane, Sheldon Patinkin, and myself. Here's what I said on that occasion:

"I'm grateful that so many friends turned up for this free lunch. I'm grateful to Andrew Alexander for paying for it, and for the good work of Kelly and Beth and the staff and casts of The Second City in making this celebration a success. I salute Sheldon and Joyce, and all of you who are here and all of those who are not here, for one reason or another.

"Our larger purpose in being here is to celebrate comedy. As any of the actors here who have gone through the agony of putting on a new show can tell you, comedy is no laughing matter. Comedy, as Herzen said, contains something revolutionary. Voltaire's laughter, he said, was more destructive than Rousseau's weeping. And who are we to argue with Alexander Herzen? He must have been right.

"Ponder this: when we at The Second City went on the attack forty years ago, Nixon was thinking of running for president—and because of our incisive comedy, he didn't get elected, did he? And then—it took some time—due to our persistence, Lawrence Welk lasted only three decades. And both of the mayors Daley seriously considered not run-

From left, Andrew Alexander, Sheldon Patinkin, and Kelly Leonard at the fortieth anniversary celebration of The Second City.

ning when they heard we were after them. Look at the world today, how we've improved it. Because of The Second City there is no more racism. War is a thing of the past, and we've eliminated poverty.

"But seriously, folks, and do let me turn serious for a moment to assure you that it is not comedy's role to change the world. The fact is, man is the only animal that laughs, and comedy's major role is to evoke the laughter that celebrates our unity as mortal creatures—we who were born into this world without our consent and must leave it the same way; we who must eat and drink, defecate, and break wind in order to live and procreate. Comedy informs us that in this respect we are not alone, that as kings and peasants, priests and penitents, we are all in the same boat, moved to find ways to deal with our fate. Our laughter is at once a protest and an acceptance of our common destiny.

"As my friend Ted Cohen said, when we as a community laugh at the same thing, it's a very special moment. It's the realization of a desperate hope: the hope that we are enough like one another to sense one another and to be able to live together.

"That is exactly why The Second City is still here after forty years. May it continue to bring us together in that hope."

Notes on Staging
Review Theatre

Preface

Some years ago I led a series of directing workshops at The Second City. From them I have extracted the material for these notes on review theatre. Some twenty directors, actors, and writers attended the sessions, and their alertness, intelligence, and skepticism play no small part in whatever virtues these notes exhibit.

Throughout the notes are a series of exercises aimed at solving various problems in the devising and staging of review theatre. I would also refer readers to Viola Spolin's book *Improvisation for the Theatre.* It is an invaluable source of exercises for many of the points covered in these notes and has influenced and inspired a generation of teachers. My own exercises follow the principles she was the first to lay down. Some of these are what I call "talking exercises," in which the give and take of discussion (in "Raising the Stakes," for example) leads to solutions. Others are for the stage, though I do try to design all my exercises with the full class participating as interactive observers. One more word about the exercises: many of them may be combined or sequenced to create scenes.

The first thing to remember in creating review theatre is

to play to the limits of your skill and intelligence, and hope it works. You must do this not out of snobbishness or romantic notions of purity. The dynamic is such that if you do not play with total commitment, you are in effect talking down to your audience. And the audience, no matter how brutish and insensitive it may be, will immediately sense that fact and won't like you for it. Believe me, if you try to outguess the audience you will not only fail, you will be doubly degraded—like the virtuous woman who decides to become a hooker, only to find that no one is buying.

I am aware that there are legions of successful hack writers who turn out B-movies and cheap novels, but I believe that those artists who consistently succeed with the public are working at the top of their skills. If their output is, in our opinion, hack work, they are nevertheless working at the top of their hack skills. They are doing the best job they can do, and they are not talking down.

What to do if you are playing to dumb audiences? It must be said gently, but in the end it boils down to: get a new audience. When you are on stage or when you are directing, you must consider the audience as being at least as intelligent as you are, perhaps more so. They are your peers, your community. If you believe in your work, hang on. Eventually you will find your audience. Sooner or later an artist gets the audience he or she deserves.

Now, a bit of inspirational violin music, please—better still, a whole orchestra. The goal of our work is not merely to entertain the audience. Good work in this genre requires too much intelligence, faith, and idealism just for that. We are not doing this only to make audiences laugh; we are here to affirm our sense of community with them and to invite them to an idea of the world. This is one of the things art does, and I use the word—art—unashamedly to describe some of our work. Some of it, maybe just a little, but some of it. Orchestra under and out.

Contents

for Notes on Staging Review Theatre

Where We Came From:
A Very Brief History of Review

Review is a stage presentation that uses short scenes of varying lengths. Add music and songs and think of it as generally comical and topical by nature. One can approach this work in many ways, but I do so through the scene as the basic building block. For me the shortest blackout and the funniest song have scenic elements. I define a scene as a short dramatic unit with a beginning, a middle, and an end. As it's used in review, it is also relevant to the community.

For our work and for that of most of our historical predecessors in review theatre, writers are not usually employed. Most of the material is devised by the cast. Hold on to that idea because it is the focus of much that we will be talking about. But first it would help us to know where we came from, to locate ourselves on a broad, unbroken continuum of theatre that stretches back more than twenty-five centuries.

The short comic scene is the oldest form of Western drama. All of us who work in variety, in sitcoms, as stand-up comedians, in circuses—all of us who present and devise the comic are the heirs of a great tradition. We have a responsibility to history when we do this work. This is not a form of ancestor worship, just an attempt to keep you from making mistakes that go back 2,500 years.

A dual aspect of human life existed from earliest times.

Coupled with the serious cults that worshiped a God, there were the comic cults that laughed at a God. Coupled with serious myths were comic ones. Coupled with heroes were the parodies of heroes. All the serious forms and concepts of human existence were transformed to a comic level.

In the same light we can identify two distinct forms of theatre. On the one hand we have that great, serious classical enterprise, the theatre of lofty and noble ideas, of tragic heroes and of important literary, often poetic, merit. It flourishes when some of the greatest creative and literary minds of an age are drawn to the drama as their means of expression.

But another form of theatre flourishes at the same time. It centers on the short comic scene and may be called the popular theatre. It is the theatre of everyday life, of laughter, of strolling players, clowns, stand-up comedians, vaudeville. It is above all a theatre without heroes—strong in satire, parody, and irony. While the classical theatre is a recurring but very rare and very brief-lived phenomenon, the popular theatre has existed in an unbroken line for 2,600 years.

We trace the beginnings of popular theatre—in fact of all Western theatre—to the sixth century B.C. in Greece. There each year, after the hard work of the harvest, the villagers "unwound" in celebrations that centered on Dionysus, the god of wine. These festivities were raucous, disorderly and irreverent, profane, rude, impudent and insolent—lots of fun.

Aristotle regarded dramatic comedy as originating in these celebrations, with a differentiation between the leader and the chorus in phallic songs. These songs were featured in the drunken processions that formed part of Dionysian festivals.

From these beginnings a ritual, serious drama branched off. As part of huge religious celebrations, Greek literary figures began to transform the religious and historic myths of their society into what we now know as classical Greek drama. The great theatre of Aeschylus, Sophocles, Euripides, and Aristophanes was born. Still, all of their plays, their entire output, were written in a period of fifty-eight years. Think of it! What is more, this great Greek canon, created over just six decades in the fifth century B.C., continued to play for about a hundred years, then disappeared from the stage for almost fifteen centuries. Imagine if there were no written theatre from the fifth century until now and you can begin to appreciate the time spans involved.

The older form of performance, the rough comedy, existed alongside the classical. Rather than seriously dealing with the myths of the community, it burlesqued gods and heroes. While one branch of the Dionysian revels grew into the ritualistic drama, another evolved as a sort of street performance involving jugglers, actors, musicians, and acrobats in cheerfully obscene sketches that lampooned not only the gods but politicians, philosophers, generals, and other public figures. These performers formed traveling troupes and they traveled light. They were vulgar, underpaid, and irreverent. And they proved to be the most imperishable form of theatre. While the classical theatre died and was reborn several times, the popular theatre existed without interruption to the present day.

The rough improvisations of the Greek traveling players were transformed into literature with the plays of Aristophanes and Menander. These begot the Roman Plautus who himself, after centuries of strolling players and troubadours, was reborn in the Italian Renaissance. Then, from Italy in the sixteenth century comedy troupes traveled to Paris and London and became the rage. Molière and Beaumarchais, Shakespeare and Ben Jonson learned from them. Royalty took them up. High and low alike adored them.

But by the end of the seventeenth century these comedians had lost both royal patronage and intellectual approval. They and the comic types they had created survived only in fairs as street players, and in a late-eighteenth-century development: the circus. A little over a hundred years ago they returned to the theatre in France in a style called vaudeville. And with the advent of the movies and television, with Chaplin, Laurel and Hardy, the Marx Brothers, Jackie Gleason, Robin Williams, John Belushi, Bill Murray, the theatre without heroes flourishes once more. Once more the comedian is king.

We are heirs to a great tradition. And most of us honor that tradition, remaining vulgar, underpaid, and irreverent. I enjoin you to hold on to two of those three qualities.

The Theoretical Basis of Our Work

Our scenes—and a case can be made that it is true of all comedy—are based on pointing out the difference between what people say and what they do, what they profess to believe and what they practice, what ought to be and what is.

If our work is the theatre without heroes, how do we deal with presidents and mayors and baseball players, the worlds of our institutions, of politics, government, and religion, and finally our everyday world of love and work and social interactions? The answer is, of course, through irony. Here are a few definitions of irony. Some of them are Webster's and some are mine.

1. An expression in which the intended meaning is the opposite of the expressed meaning.

2. A contradictory view of events, as if in mockery of the promise and fitness of things. (I like this one.)

3. The refusal to accept the professed idealism of any authority at its face value.

Always we must include ourselves, our own beliefs, our own icons, our own sins in the irony. This absents cynicism and promotes humanness. We can reach that goal only part of the time. But, wonderfully, when we do we are the most effective. When we burn at some cant or injustice, we must try to people the scene with people like ourselves. One of our directors recently staged a review with physically handicapped actors mercilessly poking fun at themselves. They were not angry. They were not asking for pity. So the show was infinitely more effective in making the audience aware of their own insensitivity. The audience was identifying with the problem. Nobody likes to call himself a villain.

Ironic truths are great levelers. Laughter makes equals of kings and commoners. That is why we are the theatre without heroes. Laughter deflates the high and mighty and gives structure to our world.

So the highest mission of our work is to provide our peers with a way of understanding, and thus in a small way controlling, their world. At The Second City our audiences and our actors are predominately young people. They come here as audience and are addressed by people their own age about all sorts of problems—growing up, leaving the nest, dealing with politics. They sit here in our theatre and achieve insights that we their peers are providing them. They take in certain truths, attitudes, and viewpoints. In so doing they annihilate some of the randomness of all that is besetting them. They now have clues to dealing with the world. They are delighted. They come here again and again for that reason.

Thus we have a true community with our audience. We speak to their concerns. We illuminate facets of their own experience that they never marked, never thought about in that way, never even named. "That's true," they say when they see their reflection mirrored on stage. "By God, that's true." And they laugh. And when they laugh, it's from delight. And they love you for it. And they give us money. So we have a heavy responsibility to them as well as a fiduciary duty to ourselves to keep telling the truth. Telling the truth is the most commercial, practical way to success.

The Elements of Review

We are indeed the theatre without heroes. The ground of our work is irony, and its basic unit is the scene. These are the types of scenes that constitute a review: blackouts, parodies, songs, relating scenes, satires, and improvised games. These are the formal units with which we build a show. Let's explore the demands of each type.

The Blackout. A blackout is a short, one-joke scene, a little filler we use to cover a costume change, to bump up the pace of a show after a scene that has ended quietly, to give some stage time to an actor who has not been seen for a while.

In content, blackouts run the gamut from sharp social comment—as with the policeman who, after gunning down a fleeing suspect, remembers to say "Freeze!"—to the delightfully funny—the evangelist who starts preaching to his captive audience in a high-rise elevator.

I have often found that the reason a particular two- or three-minute scene is not working is that it is essentially a shorter, one-joke affair that we have managed to overelaborate. By cutting it down to that one joke we often wind up with a serviceable blackout to replace an unsuccessful scene. But even in a one-joke scene, realistic behavior (good acting) matters.

Here is one of our oldest blackouts. It's called "Christian Science Reading Room." Someone once remarked about Christian Science Reading Rooms that they are always in an affluent part of town and there's never anyone in them. The scene opens with an actor answering the telephone.

> LIBRARIAN: *(on the phone)* Christian Science Reading Room, how can I help you?
> *(A Patron enters and comes downstage to browse at an imaginary shelf of books.)*
> LIBRARIAN: *(continuing on the phone)* Yes, we are open from nine to five, except on Sundays. You are very welcome. Good-bye.
> *(The Patron has found a book and carries it to a nearby chair. As he sits down the chair collapses and he falls to the floor.)*
> PATRON: This chair is broken.
> LIBRARIAN: Leave it alone, it will fix itself.

Now, there are several ways to play this. The Patron may be angry, the Librarian brusque. It works best when both actors do it mildly, peacefully, so that the fall is the only jarring element in the scene. The point is, even in a little joke scene—whether it's the doctor turning away from examining the accident victim with, "Ugh! this man's underwear is dirty," or two doctors looking up dirty words in the dictionary—authentic acting plays an important part in effectiveness. Playing the roles truthfully, no matter how brief they are, is always most effective.

Exercise: Acting in a blackout
Either with existing blackouts or with blackouts made up by the class. Have the actors present them in various styles: dramatic, realistic, etc.

Parody. This ancient form is most difficult to master, not only because of the level of skill involved but because form and content must accurately mesh.

Simply put, a parody is a scene that takes off on some existing form. Of course, it has to be a form where the reference level of the audience and the actors is the same. You cannot effectively parody something that is unfamiliar to the audience. Furthermore, it uses the elements and characteristics of a specific and established form, work, or style— such as a play, a ballet, an opera, a film, or a talk show—for the purpose of making a political or social comment.

Parody is the form in which mistakes are most common. It is not merely a matter of lampooning an existing work. First of all, the political or social content of the parody must serve a subject outside the form. The parody must be about something other than itself. The Second City did a parody of the *Pirates of Penzance* about the Chicago City Council, with the mayor as pirate chief and the aldermen as his pirates. The parody form was Gilbert and Sullivan, the subject was the attempt by the aldermen (pirates) to take over political power—an appropriate marriage of subject and form.

Sometimes we do see straight parodies of an existing form, but these are generally ineffective. Even if you have the skills to do a straight parody of the form, why do it unless it's for aficionados? If you are doing a straight ballet parody with ballet dancers, it's ballet fans who will laugh. Even then, you are parodying the eccentricities or styles of certain choreographers, dancers, or what we see as ludicrous aspects of the ballet itself. It is sure to be insider stuff.

This caution has one exception: when the original work has lofty pretensions to a high ideal which it does not earn. For example, we did a straight parody of *The Grapes of Wrath* for a television show which we called the "Grapes of Mud." It was aimed solely at the sentimentality and pretentiousness of the original. Even so, it would have been more effective had we been able to enrich it with a "war on poverty" or a "welfare reform" component.

From this we come to a second point about parody. The connection between the form and the new subject matter must be organic. This is very important. You cannot just suggest, "Let's do a Hamlet parody about the president of the United States." If the president is not a Hamlet figure in a Hamlet situation, it will not work. Chicago aldermen *are* pirates. The form and the subject matter are organically welded; they illuminate each other.

In a couple of simple ways you can determine if that organic connection is there. First, express to yourself the analogies you are making. From the previous example you might ask, "Since I'm comparing city council members to Gilbert and Sullivan pirates, is that a legitimate comparison?" In the scene we have cited the answer is yes. Second, listen to the voices of the piece. If the connection is not there you will hear two voices: the voice of the piece and the voice of the people who made the piece imposing their own viewpoint willy-nilly. I know it seems like pandering, but I also listen to the audience in these situations. The audience, of course, does not characterize its reactions, but the reactions are there. If the thing that made everyone howl in rehearsal is met with faint smiles or none; if that look of appreciative recognition is absent from their faces, you had better reexamine your basic idea.

Exercise: Parody subjects, a discussion exercise
From newspapers or magazines, select events that are high profile and interest the class. Describe them by analogy and character. "The events on this train were like a Hitchcock film." "This union fight is like Spartacus." "This presidential race is a farce comedy."
   Variation: Select a specific musical, ballet, drama, film, etc., and reverse the above process: search for events that parallel their stories. In either case, once a fit has been agreed to, keep working out the parallels until you have shaped a scene.

By the way, audiences are made uncomfortable if you pretend to speak in one voice when you are actually speaking in another, when suddenly they hear not the voice of the scene but that of the author or director. For instance, if an ending does not grow from the work but is tacked on by bringing in new information not inherent in the piece (a messenger who reveals that the girl is adopted, or "My goodness, it was all a dream!"), the audience may applaud, they may laugh, but they do not really buy it. (More about this later.) This also happens when a character launches into a political speech about social injustice. I call it the "Wherever there's a hungry man in the world, I'll be there" syndrome. Audiences do not really buy it because they sense that the author is not serving the character, he is using the character as a mouthpiece for his own protests. They do not like to be manipulated in that fashion. Serve the scene. When a scene is not working, the first thing to ask is whether the scene is speaking or whether you are using the scene to send a direct message or to speak in your own voice.

So, first, the parody must serve an idea outside the form, and, second, there must be an organic connection between your idea and the work parodied.

Point three: the parody must be executed at a high level of skill. If you dance badly in a ballet parody, sing badly in an opera parody, what is the subject of fun? Really, your own lack of skill. Since we are using parody as a vehicle to carry a message, it must be done with some skill lest the lack of skill become the message.

We parodied a Tchaikovsky ballet in a piece about Chicago police brutality in the 1968 Democratic convention. It was a nifty little number we called "Swine Lake." I brought in a ballet master who worked with us for weeks until we could achieve a respectable level of dancing. You should have seen the *pas de quatre*. Everything we did was skillful. We just did less and kept it to the skill level we could attain.

Another important thing to remember is that the wit and effect of the parody goes down as the target goes down. If you do a parody of television, it is likely to be one step worse than the television show itself.

So your parody form must be worthy because you are,

perforce, reducing it anyway. If you take something terribly silly, like a Balkan talk show, and parody it you are not making much of a point. In general, choose a high level of discourse for your parody. If your skill level is high—that is, if you are displaying some virtuosity in the parody medium— the message of the piece will be more effectively communicated.

Behavior Scenes. TV sitcoms are pale examples of what we call "behavior scenes." For those unfamiliar with The Second City, this may be a strange category. While it is essential in our work—even in outrageous scenes—to play characters of great believability, it is in behavior scenes that we come closest to written drama.

A behavior scene, first of all, deals with characters like our audiences and ourselves (as I noted earlier, if we assume in our work that our audiences are like ourselves, eventually they will be). These characters are played with as much truth as we can muster, in believable or in ordinary situations. The scenes may also deal with famous people or even people unlike ourselves, provided they are treated as ordinary people in believable situations, and provided their behavior is as realistic as we can make it.

Of course we want realistic behavior in all our scenes. But in these behavior scenes the point lies in the behavior itself; the events of the scene are a subtext. Take, for example, an unmarried couple in a scene where she wants a marriage and he doesn't—or better still nowadays, where he wants marriage and she doesn't; or a liberal family with a bigoted couple moving next door; or two people on a blind date finding they have the wrong things in common. Play them as realistically as possible. Sympathize with their dilemmas. Make the acting real enough so that the degree of audience identification with the characters is closer to that of a play than of a comedy sketch. This all may sound perilously close to not being funny. But if truthfully played and properly premised, behavior scenes evoke the most gratifying of all laughs, the laughter of recognition.

Severn Darden and Barbara Harris used to do a great behavior scene called "Blind Date." He plays a reclusive polymath, awkward with and essentially frightened of women. She, his sister, is trying to arrange a blind date for him. She takes him through the steps of the coming evening, from picking up his date to ordering dinner in a French restaurant. Earnestly he tries to behave correctly, only to fail decisively. In a down and touching ending, he decides against going through with the blind date. From point to point the scene is richly comical, but the subtext of his insecurity—his fear, actually—and her concern for him provide a profound base to the scene. More than that, these subtexts are what the scene is really about. I would give it a poor chance of appearing on television, but it scored heavily in the theatre. The scene was funny, touching, sad, human—all at the same time. That is what we call a behavior scene. And that is what we call funny.

Behavior scenes, however, are not confined to ordinary situations as long as we treat extraordinary situations as ordinary—in other words, as believable. Example: we have had several scenes that take place after an atomic attack—not, we hope, an ordinary situation, but we played them believably.

A review cannot work with more than two or three such

behavior scenes in it. The level of involvement, the intensity is too great to sustain over an entire evening. Too many such scenes and the audience feels like a Ping-Pong ball.

Most behavior scenes involve two, sometimes three, actors. In developing them I find quiet sessions the most productive, with the director and the actors in close contact exploring the possibilities of an agreed-to premise (the sister preparing her shy brother for a blind date; the married dentist in love with his hygienist). This is the most collaborative of ventures, with all involved quietly contributing. At the end of each such session I have the actors play through twice what we have done, once with quiet intensity, the second time all-out raucous.

Music and Song. In this work we have music everywhere—songs in the show, music around and under the show. Right from the start at The Second City we were blessed with musicians who actually steered and paced the work during the performance. Bill Matthieu and Fred Kaz knew when to play during a scene and when to sit out. They knew how to help a scene end, how to cover the transitions between scenes, and how to play at the beginning of scenes. The important artistic point is that the music must not lead the audience, must not tell them what to think or how they should react. The music must augment the characters and events on the stage. Of course when we started there were no electronic instruments, no synthesizers. Now one musician can achieve the most startling of polyphonic effects. But our musicians have always been resourceful. I remember when Fred Kaz spent days putting together a collection of bedpans. He would strike each one with a drumstick and eventually, when he had six or seven that satisfied him tonally, he strung them on a steel pole and taught the cast to play a song. It beat the hell out of a synthesizer—and was much funnier.

Fred and Bill also composed songs. One of the rare birds in this work is a truly funny song. I do not know that we have had ten of them in our four decades. Writing a funny lyric seems easy but is very, very difficult. For one, the song form does not bear a lot of density. Often, but not always, it is a parody, and parody rules apply. Generally the refrain carries the comic point in the form of a good punch line— "I hate liver," or "When the tide went out I found you." One of my favorite refrains was written by Nate Herman, one of our actors who is also a musician: "There's too much sex and violence on TV and not enough at home." A great refrain—unfortunately the rest of the song did not measure up to it.

And you have to give the song enough variety to last three minutes. Most of the time you end up riffing on the same point. One reason songs cannot be very dense is that people tend not to listen if they are at all hard to follow. You have to minimize the point so it fits in one or two sentences. And with any song, acting is important. With that in mind I suggest you listen to Sinatra, Crosby, or any of the great song stylists. They are actors. My precept here is, play a song like a scene. Still, it is a very difficult form. The majority of The Second City's really successful songs have been under two minutes. Sometimes it is best just to forget the AABA form. Make your point, climax, and get out. Here's one that I think works. It is called "Your Fault."

"Your Fault"
(lyric by David Rasche, music by Fred Kaz)
Scene: A cocktail singer standing at the piano. In his

hand a drink. He lights a cigarette. The piano tinkles as he speaks the opening.

SINGER: Oh my darling, my dearest. Once we were in love, so much in love. We walked together, laughed together, cried together. Then something happened between us. Something went cruelly wrong. What was it? Why did it all go bad? *(sings)*
It was your fault.
How many times I have said it?
It was your fault,
Are you too dense to get it?
You're dumb, you're just a loser in the long race.
I never really liked you in the first place—I'm not to blame.
It was your fault.
When I look back at all you have ruined
I give my head a crack *(fist to forehead).*

You may not want to face it but it is true, dear,
I'm much the better human being than you, dear.
No *mea culpa.*

You're completely to blame, can't you see?
You made all the mistakes . . . not me.
It was your fault. It was your fault. It was your fault.
(lifts glass)

I like that one. It is under two minutes and an unusual form: AAB.

Now, song and music in opera or musical theatre parodies is another matter. There again the parody rules about skill should be applied. You must sing very well, the music must be well written. I am not fond of taking a well-known song and changing the lyrics for comic effect—"There's no vinism like chauvinism," for instance. It's too easy. It's much worthier if the songs in a musical parody are original while evoking the style they are parodying. And, of course, the songs must illuminate the point you are making with your parody.

Satire Scenes. Without reference to the usual literary definitions, I distinguish between behavior scenes and satires. A behavior scene can have satiric elements, but its comedy rises from the conduct of its characters, just as a satire scene must be played realistically but derives its primary humor from ideas. And there are other differences.

We defined a behavior scene as dealing with realistic characters in ordinary situations. In contrast, a satiric scene either portrays unbelievable or stereotypical characters in familiar situations, or ordinary people in unbelievable situations and the extension of the resulting scene into the absurd. The aim is to criticize social attitudes. The most famous of these, of course, is Jonathan Swift's "Modest Proposal," in which he solved at one stroke the problems of hunger, poverty, and overpopulation by proposing in a most serious and justifiable way that we eat babies. Everything about his proposal is rational and logical, except his absurd solution. Were we to do a scene about this, the acting would be realistic but the central identification would be with the satiric point, not with the behavior.

No subject, from AIDS to rape, cannot be acceptably dealt with in a satiric scene, if not directly then in some aspect of the subject. You might deal with the excessive reactions to the subject or, as in this Second City scene called "Robbery," to some other tangential aspect. Here the setting is a courtroom. Present are a man in the witness chair, a female judge, and a female lawyer.

LAWYER: *(to judge)* Thank you, your honor. *(to witness)* Now, Mr. Johnson, would you like to tell me exactly where you were at the time of the alleged robbery?

WITNESS: Sixty-third and Stony Island.

L: That is well known as a dangerous neighborhood. Do you usually make it a habit to walk around that neighborhood late at night—by yourself?

W: No, ma'am, I was visiting my friend at the University of Chicago, and I was going to get my car.

L: I see, and why didn't one of your friends accompany you to your car?

W: They never leave campus, you see.

L: Mr. Johnson, would you like to tell me what was said at the time of the alleged robbery?

W: Yes, a man came up to me with a gun and said, "Stick 'em up and give me all your money."

L: I see. And what did you do?

W: I stuck 'em up and gave him all my money.

L: *(incredulous)* You handed the money over?

W: Well, yes. I . . .

L: Did you put up any kind of fight, Mr. Johnson?

W: Well, no.

L: You just gave the money to this man?

W: You see . . .

L: Your honor, please direct the witness to answer.
   (The Judge and the Witness exchange glances. The Witness capitulates.)

W: Yes, I just gave him the money.

L: Mr. Johnson, would you say there was any pleasure involved in giving him the money?

W: Certainly not.

L: Did you enjoy it at all?

W: No! No!

L: Nevertheless, you did just hand it over without protest?

W: I . . . you see . . .

L: Mr. Johnson, how were you dressed at the time of the robbery?

W: Well, it was a formal party. I had on my Armani suit, I guess.

JUDGE: Armani, is that Giorgio Armani, Mr. Johnson?

W: Yes, Giorgio Armani.

L: Wouldn't you say that is a very expensive line of clothing?

W: Well, it is a nice suit.

L: Wouldn't you say that you were screaming money, that you were exuding wealth? Mr. Johnson, do you know what that type of clothing does to a robber? Furthermore, Mr. Johnson, wouldn't you agree that you have a history of giving money away?

W: Well, I . . .

L: That you are a well-known philanthropist?

W: I give to certain needy causes.

L: Aren't you an easy mark for any charity that asks you?

W: Now just a second . . .

L: Well now, let's see if we have all this correct. You were walking around in a strange neighborhood, late at night, in flashy clothing that just screamed, "Come and get me," and you have a well-known history of giving money away. Is all of that correct?

w: Well, yes, but . . .

l: The defense rests, your honor.

About a third of the way through the scene the audience gets the point that Johnson's situation is parallel to that of a rape victim with an unsympathetic policeman. This is not a funny scene about rape but a satiric look at how the police treat rape victims. The absurdity of the content creates for the audience an identification with the point of the scene and not, as in a behavior scene, with the characters. Here is an ordinary character in an unbelievable situation that extends into the absurd. As noted, the other satiric mode places unreal characters in familiar situations. Gulliver among the Lilliputians: an ordinary character in an unreal situation. Dr. Strangelove: a farfetched character in a believable situation.

These are hard-edged scenes that do not usually depend on identifying with the characters but on identifying the situation and appreciating its absurdity. But, again, that does not mean the characters are not played realistically. If in our rape scene the characters were to play it silly and not observe proper courtroom procedures, it would not work as well. Only the central point can be absurd; everything else is realistic.

The playing must be real because it adds to the impact of your satiric point. Swift's "Modest Proposal" was couched in serious language and proceeded with proper rhetoric. This essential point is true of all the forms: parodies, scenes, even blackouts. It is one of the reasons The Second City has survived. Many people, who should know better, think that to have a funny scene you must act funny. Not true. You must strive to be real.

You will notice from our example that in its own way it

turns the world upside-down. One path to developing scenes like this is the what-if mode. What if a rape victim were a man? What if the head of the insane asylum were crazy? What if we solved hunger through cannibalism? While this process is too subtle and slow for a group exercise, I would advise carrying this what-if mind-set through a couple of sessions of newspaper readings.

Games and Improvisation. Games are fun. The reason we call them theatre games is because that's what they are. There is an established set of rules, known to all the players and the audience, and a goal. The spectators witness the players attempt to reach that goal according to the rules. Viola Spolin's books have lots of games, ranging from "make-a-song," in which the actors make up a song on a theme and in a style specified by the audience, to "first-line, last-line," in which the actors start and end an improvised scene with lines called out by the audience.

We use games in a show under certain conditions. First, if we are playing a game, it is clearly a game. We say so. "Now," we say from the stage, "we, the actors, and you, the audience, are going to have some fun together."

Next, we avoid turning the game into a mere display of technical virtuosity. Every game can be played at the behavior level. Still, games are essentially presentational and showing off. For these reasons I feel it is a bit of a cop-out to use them in the show. But sometimes they are an easy way to get a nice energy boost, a change of pace. Sometimes a game may give an actor who is light in the show something to do. Sometimes you are stuck for a scene and everyone has run out of inspiration. Sometimes the director is lazy.

I have a running argument with devotees of improvisation (I passionately dislike the word "improv") about its viability and value as a presentational form. It is highly limited—momentarily interesting as a game but scarcely sustainable night after night. For one, most of the time it fails as a coherent theatre piece. When it does succeed its virtue most often lies not in its concise expression, nor in relevant content or balance of scenic structure, but in its game aspect. The audience watches it as a display of skills, like juggling, pantomime, or stage combat. They know the rules, and they are interested in how the actors achieve their goals. As an "entertainment" it is often fun to watch. But the deeper value of any expression does not depend on how it is achieved but what is expressed. Whether it is made up on the spot, found under a stone, or written down is finally not important. It is the scene itself that matters, its artistic quality and not its origins. How much better a scene can speak if it is worked on, shaped, edited, with its prolixities curbed, its self-indulgences excised. Worst of all to me, presenting pure improvisation inevitably results in the elevation of form over content and the player over the play.

I know that many actors believe they can improvise in front of audiences better scenes than anyone can write for them, and that what results is unique and can be achieved in no other way. To them I ask, why does it fail so often, and why should I forgive that? They frequently reply that it is a new form and takes time to develop. But this is not true. It is older than writing. And even the masters—the *dell'arte* people—codified their work and narrowed it to specific characters and comic turns that they used over and over again. Some very wise heads claim a unique, an almost metaphysical virtue in pure improvisation with an audience present.

And I admit to seeing some wonderful things happen in that situation. But I have also seen enough terrible things—and that is most of the time—to want to polish and prune. I just do not believe it is viable for audiences or actors to successfully improvise night after night on a regular schedule.

But for our purposes the improvisation issue is less important than the other matters we discuss here. From acting to scene structure, from blocking to the use of the environment, certain principles apply no matter how you approach the work. And we can agree on the kinds of humor we aim for. It differs from that of stand-up comedians or of sitcom writers who look for a laugh on every line. They manipulate the laugh, setting up the joke, delivering the punch line, doing everything short of leaning in and saying, "Get it?" When we are working at our best on stage, our audiences are seldom belly-laughing; they are affirming, recognizing. "Oh, yeah!" they are saying. "That's true." And that reaction comes from believable characters who are relating to one another and with whom the audience identifies.

Writing, Design, Props, Costume

Acting as Writing. In our work, most of the writing is done by the actor. By writing I do not necessarily mean setting pen to paper. We arrive at most of our scenes through improvisation and polish them in formal rehearsals. They are preserved in print or picture only after they are set. Still, whether we improvise a scene or set it down we are, in a way, writing—conveying information and advancing a story. Someone once observed that in one sense all music is singing. In a similar sense all acting is writing. Any legitimate gesture by an actor forwards the action, conveys information, and advances the story. For example, if, as an actor in a scene, I look at my watch, I am doing something quite complex. First of all, I am doing it in character. A doctor may very well look at his watch differently from a carpenter, a twenty-year-old from a forty-year-old, an introvert from an extrovert, a man from a woman, a cautious person from a rash one.

Now, add the reason I am looking at my watch, a reason that has to do with story. I am late for an appointment. I am impatiently waiting for someone. I am bored with my wife. I am timing something. More information: Is it a new watch? Is it unreliable? Do I need glasses? And so forth. In that simple action of looking at a watch, a good actor can convey a world of information. That is why for the short comic scene, in which, unlike a play, the actor does not have two hours to build a character and tell a story, you must have really skilled actors. They may do less, but what they do must be forceful and true, and everything they do helps write the story.

Here is another example of simple actions conveying a wealth of information: sitting down in a chair. What can an actor convey by the everyday act of sitting in a chair? Fatigue, depression, getting down to business, professional standing, and—this must not be neglected—age. A forty-year-old sits down in a chair differently from a twenty-year-old—more deliberate, less secure about the geography of the chair.

Exercise: Playing age, playing profession
The scene is a bus stop or the outside of a department store just before opening. The director secretly assigns an age and a profession to each actor. Two actors enter,

one at a time, and stop to wait for the bus, or for the store to open. They are to exchange a few lines of dialog but are not to mention their ages or professions. The rest of the class then guesses their ages and professions. The director corrects any mistakes. The next pair repeats the exercise.

Designing the Set. In the same way that acting is writing, so is design. The Second City uses no sets, but whether it is our bare stage, where the setting is totally imagined, or a theatre stage housing elaborate scenery, the actors have the same responsibility. They must "see" and react to the setting. In our theatre we "design" our rooms and the objects in those rooms by miming them, which means of course that the actors must all "see" the same thing in the same position or the audience will be uncomfortable. Working in this way, we learned something important that applies equally to our work and to the conventional theatre, to the most simple or the most elaborate of settings. If the actor does not "see" the space and does not react to it physically, then the space does not truly exist for the audience, even if there is an elaborate set on stage. Thus when we enter a room on stage we must see the ceiling, the walls, the paintings on the walls, the furniture, the floor—feel the volume of the room.

In what sense is design too a form of writing? The actor in the set is always transmitting information. For instance, suppose, as an actor, you are one of two people entering a room. The room is in your house, and the other actor has never been there before. Each of you will look at the room differently (the stranger will probably look at the ceiling first), and your bodies will react to it differently. You will also scan it differently if you are there for a purpose. You will react differently if it is a large room or a small one, etc.

In other words, when it comes to design the actor has a dual job: creating the setting and conveying his or her relationship to that setting. Is it the first time you have walked into that space? Is it a large and awesome space? Where are you coming from when you enter the space? Where are you going when you leave it? What objects are in the space? Are there windows? In a play the designer creates the space, and the actors by their behavior complete it. In our work the actors both design the space and complete it.

Exercise: Creating the space
Actors in pairs or threes. Start a scene (first three or four lines) having pre-planned the space—its character, size, furniture, and meaning to the characters in the scene. The rest of the class will then attempt to describe the space.

The details of design, the setting and the furniture, come from an agreement among the actors. If they are not together on this point, the audience will be confused, the set will be nonfunctional, and the scene will very likely be maimed. This is a crucial point in staging and particularly in public improvisation. There must be scenic agreement, not necessarily in advance but certainly in practice. The shape, furnishings, and details of a space must be conveyed by one actor to another through behavior in the scene. For the scene to be maximally effective, actors must watch one another for clues to the look of the room and the objects in the room, especially if they are in the wings waiting to go on. If an actor is entering a room and, while heading straight for an-

Meagen Fay restraining Jim Belushi—not an unusual sight on The Second City stage.

other actor sitting in a chair, walks through the imaginary table on which the first actor had set his imaginary drink, the players have lost some authority with the audience. And by not "feeling" the room the actor has missed an opportunity to enrich the scene. The Second City uses no design elements: just a bare stage, six chairs, and a few props. So it is useful in rehearsal to work out these imaginary spaces and their imaginary furnishings and props in some detail.

Walk-throughs with the actors are essential—working with the spaces and reacting to them, handling the objects, giving life to all these imaginary things through their actions.

Exercise: Objects in spaces
Again, break into teams of twos or threes. The teams confer on setting up a room with at least five objects in it: TV set, bar, picture on the wall, etc. They play a short scene with each actor "using" each object in the course of playing the scene without referring to or naming the object. At the same time, as in the preceding exercise, they delineate the space itself. The rest of the class then names the objects and describes the room.

The audience will not only mark everything you do as an actor in a scene, they will remember it at some subconscious level. The audience will remember where you set down an imaginary glass. They will remember how full it is. They have a kinesthetic sense that registers these details. If you pick up that glass six inches from where you set it down several minutes ago, they know it. They may not be aware of what's disturbing them, but they do feel it, and it's a little wrench in their universe. You have lost some authority.

Props. Since we usually have the option, the question arises, When do you use real objects and when do you mime them? Personally I try not to use real objects, but sometimes they help the scene. My rule is, if you are dealing with both real and imaginary objects, do not mix them up if they are of the same class. Don't use a real billfold and imaginary money. Don't light an imaginary cigarette with a real match or a real cigarette with an imaginary lighter. On the other hand, if you have a real cigarette and a real match, you must have a real ashtray. You can see how this becomes a problem. Keep the real objects to a minimum and do not mix and match.

But your object work must be unobtrusive: simple and short. If I see one more actor miming a telephone with his thumb and little finger spread apart while he talks for two minutes, or drinking interminably from an imaginary glass with his thumb laid alongside his lower lip, I will run screaming from the theatre. The imaginary object should serve the scene the way everything else serves the scene. It should not call attention to itself. You may remember the Alan Arkin scene in which he played Noah. In it he handles a telephone beautifully. He has called up God and he is making nothing of the telephone, just a small gesture. The telephone soon disappears, and we could care less. Any gesture or motion that goes on for more than a moment starts to take over the scene. If you are an actor sitting in a rocking chair, rocking and knitting, these two activities if prolonged will very soon become the focus of the audience's attention and will dominate anything else that is going on.

Costumes. In my experience, elaborate and extensive costumes do not add anything but problems to our work. We depend on the suggestion of costume. As in our character work, some of the actor's own person shows through.

In one sense it's a question of communication. "Less is more" has a certain beauty about it. At the point where a costume stops giving new information, it becomes ornament. If you play a policeman, a hat, perhaps a jacket, is enough. You do not need striped pants and a leather belt or even a gun. If, as a businessman, you have a suit jacket and a fedora, it is not entirely necessary to have matching socks, wing-tip black shoes, tie, and matching handkerchief. (You would also have a hard time getting ready for the next scene where you play a cop.) Usually, when I do a show, I start out thinking I need a lot of costumes, and then I start eliminating things. The show is actually better without a lot of it, and cheaper too. In a funny way, full costume is limiting. The character is imprisoned in the costume—overdefined.

One bit of costume that speaks volumes is eyeglasses. From wire rims to sunglasses, from tortoise shells to severe black, glasses convey more, ounce for ounce, than any other prop. Hats are a close second. Often a hat can adequately stand in for a complete costume.

Actors sometimes come on stage fully costumed, certain of what that costume represents in terms of the character— only to find that the audience has a completely different feeling about it. The costume may be more interesting to them than the character.

Should all the actors in a review wear the same thing as a basic costume? I do insist on the actors being neat and well turned out. A bunch of bohemians getting together to do a show, while it may be attractive to some audiences, turns off most of them as well as sending the wrong message. You must have a certain authority on the stage as indicated by your dress. When The Second City first began, the men dressed in identical corduroy suits and the women in black dresses. If I recall, that changed when we hit the 1970s and the very idea of uniformity became anathema. So now we set a few standards: neutral colors, pressed trousers, clean shirts, shaves, no gum. Mustaches are no problem, but beards handicap facial mobility. No blue jeans. Neat neutrality.

Running Orders

Each of the types of scenes that go to make up a review carries its own kind of energy, length, and acting style, its own proper balance between form and content. (Too often we see blackout ideas played as long scenes or vice versa, but that's another story.) These varying characteristics of scene types influence the show's running order. I cannot overemphasize the importance of running order to the success of a show. At The Second City we deal with a menu of twenty to twenty-five scenes. Put them in one order and the show is dull. Put them in another and the show zips along. In the end, much of the process is intuitive, but there are certain guidelines.

First, an overview. Let's assume a show of two acts. This is not God-given, but from our experience an intermission in a show of disparate scenes is welcome. (Some cynics would add that this helps sell more drinks.) And it seems to work best when the two acts are uneven. The first act can be longer because the novelty of the experience permits it. The audience is with you, they can endure more, they are still full of anticipation. By the second act they are saying, "Dazzle me." A longer first act also allows the audience to get to know more of the actors.

Make an exception to this if the audience is uninitiated. A shorter first act tips them as to what the review form is, so we can be indulgent in the second act and they are right with us.

The Opening Scene. To start a show we need either a full-cast scene to introduce the actors or a series of blackouts to do the same thing. The opening starts to plant them in the minds of the audience. That's important because part of the audience's joy is to identify and marvel at the actors as they change roles throughout the evening. The sooner they begin to know them, the better. If they must wait a scene or two to see a specific actor, you have delayed the process with that actor until then.

But the opening scene has another important function: to establish your credentials. It should be intelligent, it should display the actors' skills, and it should have some of the elements of what you are about: political, behavioral, ironic, bright. It should have some substance to it, not a "Hello, how are you, welcome to our show, la dee da." It should communicate the kind of theatre you want—an intelligent theatre doing work you can be proud of. The audience will be guided by that. The opening scene—actually the entire first act—establishes your tone, your intellectual level, the respect you have for the work and the audience. This theatre is not aimed at mindless entertainment. You can turn on the television and get that.

So you open the show with full cast and high energy. Then some short funny stuff followed by what I call the center boost—a real power surge in the middle of the first act, a high-energy physical scene or a song or a parody, followed by a leave-'em-cheering end of the act. The second act can start quietly, then again a center boost, then a three-scene rush to the climax. That's the shape. Now here are some other running-order considerations.

Frequency of Appearance. Few actors believe this, but appearance in every scene hurts the actor and hurts the show. Conversely it also hurts the show if an actor is "light"—that is, not seen for long periods of time.

Most actors' egos do not allow them to understand that the audience wearies of seeing them in scene after scene. Being absent from the stage at intervals is a virtue. Somehow, if only by fiat, you must establish that principle. Worst is when you have an actor finishing a terrific scene that has been strong, well acted, and involving. The scene ends, the lights come up, and you see the same actor as another character. The audience, still bemused by the enchantment of the previous scene, does not wish immediately to see that actor again as someone else. They must first get rid of a residual memory of the scene before. They see the actor riding off into the sunset, and then he's saying, "Hi honey, I'm home." It's jarring.

Revealing Talents. In the course of a show, any newly revealed skill by an actor is exciting. One of the unmarked points of this work, one of the things that delights an audience, is when an actor who has been amusing them, absorbing them, and making them laugh, then juggles, plays the guitar, sings, reveals another talent. This cannot be as a presentational or show-off device but as an integral part of a scene. If the people who made them laugh are suddenly dancing like Nijinski, the audience thinks that's great—and it *is* great. So don't shoot your talent wad all at once. If your actors can play musical instruments, if they can whistle, dance, juggle, recite the Gettysburg Address backward— whatever, it's all usable and should be revealed over time.

But remember that it must serve the scene and the show in context.

Subject Matter. Too many scenes on the same subject can obviously be a problem. Although randomness of themes and subject matter is at the heart of review, all who do this work are eventually tempted to fill in the dots—"Wouldn't it be great to do one show about a single topic: love, politics, etc.?" Unfortunately it does not work in this form, at least in any organic way. Why? Because in the classical theatre of long forms you do not follow themes, you follow characters from whose destinies grow the themes. This mandates a constancy of character and its development over time, a procedure not applicable to the review form. I am often asked what would happen if you kept the same characters throughout? We have tried that. You wind up with what I call a salami work—from it you can extract any scene without hurting the whole. (You may be able to do that here and there in a Shakespeare play, but not often.) This means that you are either missing a necessary structural progression, or you must add an inevitable sequence of actions and a subplot— and lo and behold, you have written a play. But in order to write a play by combining improvised scenes, you would need a playwright to order and structure and—there goes the review form.

Pace and Dynamics. If you have a down ending to a scene, the next scene should generally open at high energy. Look at the beginnings and ends of scenes and try to vary and contrast them. Among other things, a show in this work is an ordering of energies—I mean physical energy in the scene: screaming, weeping, belly-laughing, gun shots, movement. If you do three behavior scenes (that tend to be slow-paced with thoughtful endings) back to back in a show, it is too demanding for an audience, too demanding for you. Use blackouts for pacing and for breaking up longer scenes.

Developing Scenes

Looking for the Irony. Some of us are funnier than others, but we all can use approaches to the world that will result in scenes. The question is, How do you look for the irony and how do you transform it to the stage? There are many ways to do it. Here are some that work for me.

One way is to transform a large subject or a world situation into its effect on ordinary people in our community. Almost always an irony crops up.

For example: One of our recent casts, for some unknown reason, was predominantly Irish, so the "troubles" in Ireland came up for consideration. How should we deal with the Irish situation? Should we put Irishmen on stage? Should we set it in Ireland? Using the method of transforming a world situation into our own experience, we came up with the setting of a local Irish bar. Our central character was an Irish-American militant, ready for those guys in Ireland to kill and be killed, ready for the hunger strikers to hold out to the end.

It was a great setting for the transformation of a large subject—troubled Ireland—into its effect on ordinary people in our community. A "democratic" American was advocating violence. A man living in luxury was quite ready for others to bleed and die.

Now that was the setting. But how would we address the

Catholic-Protestant situation directly? Where was the scene? Now we raised the stakes by introducing other characters: a Protestant hooker whom our Catholic militant fancied, the militant's boss who was on the other side.

Why did we deal with the Irish situation in this way and not directly? First of all, we are not Irish. If we populated the scene with characters in Ireland, we would be observing them externally. Second, the situation is too sad and too strong to pretend we are Irish. But the irony of such a sad situation being used by some middle-class Irish-American for his own aggrandizement and free-floating militancy does apply to our society. The very sadness of the event lends more irony to this man's reactions. And, as a bonus, if we ourselves were sensitive enough to the situation in Ireland, we captured some of the elements of that conflict.

Another way of creating scenes by looking for the irony is to transform famous or accomplished people involved in big events into ordinary people in ordinary situations. Example: At the same time we were discussing the Irish scene, we were confronted with a major league baseball strike. Here were millionaires going on strike like ordinary workers. So we decided to treat them like ordinary workers. We set up a baseball family scene in which all of the concerns were the same as if our baseball celebrity were a day laborer working for some schlock employer and fulfilling his union obligations. Picket lines with millionaires arriving in their Mercedes. Strikebreakers. Striker's kids and their problems with schoolmates, etc.

A variation of this is to place people in everyday situations outside their fields, but where their fields are involved. Example: A Supreme Court justice at dinner with her family, having to adjudicate a dispute that involves unsettling revelations. A lawyer visiting a doctor he just sued for mal-practice.

Exercise: Transforming events and people—looking for the irony
Full-class discussion. Using a newspaper, select a series of national and international events and situations and discuss transforming them into local concerns. Next, from news stories take well-known personalities and place them in mundane, real-life situations.

The question of neutrality does arise. Irony takes no sides except in its application. Should we use it then as a tool for discourse that is biased toward our own point of view? Of course. There the consideration is integrity and truthfulness. But we must strive to be evenhanded. The more credible we make each side, the more we illuminate. On the abortion question, for example, we could point out the anomalies in the pro-life position: the right of the fetus to bear arms, that's one. On the pro-choice side we could also deal with equivalent militant tendencies. To repeat one truth: the great ironists of history invariably send up their own class. Who better than a liberal to send up liberals, or a conservative to do the same for conservatives?

Turning the World Upside-down. Another way to invent scenes is to turn things upside-down. Take good for bad, and vice versa. The following exercise can sharpen this way of thinking.

Exercise: Editorials
Set up a TV editorial situation. Select a number of so-

cial or political problems: crime, drugs, teenage pregnancy. Have the actors, one by one, deliver an editorial treating these as virtues, explaining why they are good for society.

This approach often leads to full-scale scenes. In developing the rape scene that we used as an example of satiric approaches, we asked the simple question, "What if the rape victim were a man?" Turning the situation upside-down led to the scene.

Another way of turning the world upside-down is to juxtapose unlikely elements: Plato's Academy for advertising executives; Einstein courting Marilyn Monroe. In looking for the irony, you cannot always find it by approaching the subject head-on. But if you transform the unusual to the everyday, turn the everyday upside-down, or bring unlikely subjects together, the ironic point will often stare out at you and the scene will present itself. When we are working on a new show, I always tell my actors to take in the world around them from an ironic point of view. Read the newspapers, watch how people behave in public situations, and apply the things we have been talking about. Diligent practice results in this approach becoming second nature.

Raising the Stakes. Here is an actual transcript from a workshop on "raising the stakes." I include it here because it graphically illustrates the workings of the process.

SAHLINS: Today we are going to work on a process I call "raising the stakes."
CLASS: Is this about cattle breeding?

s: One more of those and I will banish you to stand-up's hell. No, this is premised on the theory that the more you reach for in a scene—the more intelligence, the more complexity, the more relating—the better and more interesting the scene. Furthermore it's a method for actually developing scenes. When you came in today, I asked you to write down a real-life situation or transaction. I have those in this bowl, and I'll fish one out at random. Good. The subject is "borrowing money." Right. Borrowing money. Here's a wonderful aspect of our work. Presto! We can raise the stakes by asking simple questions. Characters?

c: Loan officer and bank customer.

s: Nothing wrong with that. Let's try for something more intricate.

c: Poor friend, rich friend.

s: Better for purposes of our exercise. We could raise the stakes in the bank situation, but with poor friend, rich friend, there's a built-in complexity. We are speaking not only about borrowing money but now friendship is involved. What other kind of relationship can they have?

c: Brothers.

s: Good. A new set of considerations. Sibling problems. Family affairs. Any others?

c: Brothers-in-law.

s: Great, because we can raise the stakes with two more characters who are . . . ?

c: The sisters.

s: You've got it. Look, we are just starting and see what we have: poor sister, rich sister, sibling stuff all over the place. Poor brother-in-law, maybe henpecked, pushed by his wife—or maybe the other way around: rich guy henpecked. Where are they?

c: Rich couple's home.

s: Good. Where else could they be. Someplace that mandates activity?

c: Health club.

s: Good. Higher stakes by the minute. Heath fads. Dieting. Sports. What about professions, politics?

c: Poor couple are right-wingers, rich couple are intellectuals, liberals.

s: Good. Often better to play against type. Look how far we've come and we aren't even borrowing money yet. I want you to notice one important thing: we always raised the stakes not by dealing with the subject of borrowing money but by tending to the characters. The distinction I like is that between the newscast on "Saturday Night Live" and that on "SCTV." On SNL they will show you a picture of the president and make a joke. On SCTV they may tell the same damn joke but the focus is on the relationship between the passive and dominant newscasters. The joke is still there, but the behavior is primary. You are not merely saying, "Ha ha, what a good joke about the president," you are identifying a power situation between two people, which raises the stakes.

All of these details, all of this raising of the stakes, is aimed only at making the relationships more interesting and more lifelike. We are not dealing with the substance of the scenes so much as creating the tools we will use to go into the scenes, tools to explore the believable encounters among people.

This is especially difficult to achieve when improvising, because of the complexity of the work. There are too many things to think about. As directors you must instill these points until they are habits. Actors should raise the stakes as part of their equipment. They should create environments. They should tell the truth. They should know who they and the rest of the characters are and what they want. They should tend to their space, costumes, and props. If they can get into the habit of consistently doing these things, they will be free to focus on the scene. That is what makes a good actor and why you will be a good director if your actors do those things.

Summarizing, then, here is what you can do to raise the stakes.

Add characters. In "borrowing money," when we added the sisters it was a quantum raise. Not that we could not have developed a two-person scene with raised stakes, but the sisters create all sorts of wonderful possibilities: sibling rivalry, marrying well or for money, humiliation. You could riff on that for a long time. One caution: do not add a character unless it is a functional move. For example, if you have two cops and a suspect, pay attention to the dynamic between the two cops. If they are interchangeable, just use one or, better still, give the two of them differing wants and characteristics.

Change or enrich the environment. This means adding more detail to an existing environment. Changing is often more important. If you set the "borrowing money" scene in the poor couple's living room you have a different dynamic than setting it in the rich couple's living room. In either case we add details not for color but to promote action.

Increase the intelligence and self-awareness of the characters. I don't mean that all of your characters must have an encyclopedic reference level, but they must be bright and aware. See if you can change a character to one who is more intelligent. If you deal with uncomprehending characters, the scene is much less likely to pay off structurally. And it is much less likely to create identification with our audience. The more the characters comprehend about their situation, the richer will be the scene. This is as true in our work as it is in Greek tragedy.

You might think it's a little far-fetched to speak of our work in the same breath as Sophocles. I truly believe the same principles apply. If you have characters who don't know what's going on, the scene will most likely end precisely at the point where it should have begun—with the comprehending of the problem by the characters. Always ask how much your characters know, and make sure they know and express the permitted maximum.

Increase the complexity of the characters. Along with intelligence, we owe our characters another attribute. It is easy to create a villainess who is only a villainess, or a saint without blemishes. But it's worthier and more interesting to endow an unsympathetic character with human qualities that help us understand what it is in ourselves that can tolerate evil or error—or what we should really fight against. Whenever you have target characters that you want to criticize or ridicule, make them worthy targets. If you play a reactionary politician as a total jerk, that's too easy. If you make him bright, patriotic, and kind to his family, you're in a better place. A Second City scene in a bar illustrates this. Here's a man who beats his wife. But we see too that he loves his wife, that beating her is an inchoate, perverse expression of his love. This is much more interesting than dealing with violence toward women as the action of an unmitigated brute—much more horrifying, actually. Make your character complex, even self-contradictory. It's a great stake-raiser.

Other simple things can be done in this regard. Give the character a profession. The moment the actor has a profession he is outfitted with technical terms, attitudes, and background. I have often been able to improve a scene by asking an actor what he does for a living. Ask him to recite his history: what does he do, how old is he, did he piss against the sun when he was six years old?

Here's something that will save you a lot of time and energy. It is covered by the word "associate."

s: Coming back to our theme of borrowing money, what comes to mind?

c: Banks, Mafia, mortgages.

c: Reaganomics, the presidency, income disparity.

s: You've got it. Now start personifying and free-associating and pretty soon you have a sizable menu. Anyone out there who can raise the stakes of this discussion by thinking of other ways of raising the stakes?

c: You can give the characters in the scene a difficulty to overcome that is outside the scene.

s: Such as?

c: It's 105 degrees out there, and the characters have to cope with that.

s: Physical difficulties. Good. It gives the scene an enormous energy.

c: Almost anything that personalizes the characters will help in emotionally involving the audience.

s: Give me an example.

c: Your example—a loan officer and a would-be borrower. You personalize that by making them related to each other. Say they are brothers. There's a personal as well as a professional investment.

s: Good. That gives us many, many directions in which to take the scene.

Exercise: Raising the stakes
Divide the class into pairs. Have each pair start a scene.
Stop the scene for a full-class discussion on raising the
stakes. Continue the scene accordingly. If it involves
more actors, add them. The director should stop the
scene from time to time to continue raising the stakes.
Repeat the process with each pair.

One of your key jobs as a director is to create and maintain standards—intellectual standards, acting standards, scene-construction standards—that are worthy and at the highest level. The only limits are your own limitations. Yes, you are circumscribed by the actors' limitations, but you can overcome them if you encourage the actors to raise the stakes and obey these other strictures. We have done shows that are smarter than the actors in them only because I raised the stakes. We all have a responsibility to the work and to the tradition. It is easy for all of us to accept the cheap if it works, and it often does. But then you won't sleep easy.

Reference Level. One of the joys of this work is that as an actor you can use yourself wholly. Everything you have learned and experienced, every talent you have can become part of the work. The more you have to give, the more you should give. This does not mean that we use reference level to show the audience how clever we are. But generally we deal not with new ideas and passing events that come and go with the newspaper headlines, but rather with things that have troubled us over many centuries—for which we use the newspaper headlines as a starting point for our discussion. To repeat, you must consider the audience at least as bright and as well-read as you are, perhaps brighter, and you must approach them at the top of your knowledge. Among other things, it's a simple matter of respect. Your actors must believe they are always addressing their peers and perhaps their superiors, that they owe them respect for which, if given, they shall be repaid.

Opening the Scene. Like a play, a scene has a discernible beginning, a middle, and an end. Most of the mistakes in scene construction come at the beginning and are the most costly. Here I would like to introduce a technical term, the "beat." A beat is a passage in a scene that embodies a discrete unit of action. The opening beat might be followed by the mother's entrance beat, then the serving dinner beat, etc. It is a useful concept for locating a section of the scene and for determining if the scene is balanced—that is, whether a particular section of a scene is doing its job in advancing the action.

The opening beat is the exposition that corresponds to the exposition of a play. It is the foundation of the scene. If it does its job properly, the audience is informed and involved, and the scene is off and running. The opening beat must convey specific, explicit information in as highly compressed a manner as possible.

1. Who are the characters, and what is their relationship with one another? Here relationship can mean kinship, business, or social connections: brothers, client-attorney, lovers, friends, boss and employee, teacher and student.

2. Where are they? Inside, outside, at a specific location: the office, home, the Grand Canyon, etc.

3. What do they specifically want from one another? The word "specifically" aims at eliciting the particular. "You want love" can be specifically translated to "Let's go to bed" or "Will you marry me?" "You want sympathy" can be specifically translated to "I have no place to go. May I stay with you?" (This last may be an example of one want concealed by another. "May I stay with you?" can also have the hidden agenda of "I want to seduce you.") As we saw earlier, if the hidden agenda is so poorly hidden as to be apparent to the audience, the actor must respond to the hidden and not the manifest agenda. Otherwise we are dealing with awful fiction; we are behind the audience.

My examples have dealt with the wants of one of the characters to which another actor must respond. But more interesting scenes occur when both characters have strong wants which can then be used for trading.

A: I'd like to go to bed with you.
B: I want to get married.

This is more interesting if A is a woman, or if both A and B are the same sex.

Answers to these questions constitute the opening beat, and the more quickly they can be communicated the better. The drama moves forward when this information has been given. It does not have to be baldly stated and often should not be, but as a general rule, the quicker the exposition, the livelier your scene.

There are some who object to saying everything right away. But I believe the scene starts only after we have the facts—not everything, just the facts, all the facts. A scene is not information, it is actions based on information. If you conceal relevant information merely to fool the audience or to create some sort of tension, it is not only a cheat, it is dull. Exposition should be short, sharp, specific—it could be even one line. Yes, you can sometimes get all the relevant information needed to start a scene in one line. We have often played that game. My favorite is in four words. Curtain up on two men sitting on opposite sides of the desk. One of them is looking at a report. The other says, "Doctor, will I live?"

Four words, five syllables, and we have fulfilled the three requirements of an opening. We know where we are, we know who the characters are, and we know the problem. Four words and we are off and running.

The opening that dawdles or is allusive can be interesting, but never as interesting as the actions that take place once we have information. Let me take a scene that could start with "Doctor, will I live?" and show you how it would start with unskilled people or in many improvisations.

Scene: Man in a white coat seated alone at his desk. He reads a report, shakes his head, and presses his intercom.

DOCTOR: Nurse Riley, would you send in the next patient?

NURSE: *(offstage)* Yes, Dr. James.

(timid knock at the door)

DOCTOR: Come in.

(Mr. Smith enters, obviously anxious)

DOCTOR: Hello, Mr. Smith. How are you feeling?

SMITH: *(bravely)* You tell me, you're the doctor.

DOCTOR: Sit down, Mr. Smith, I have something to tell you.

SMITH: I think at this time I'd prefer standing.

DOCTOR: Mr. Smith, you have hypolepidosus.

SMITH: No! Doctor, will I live?

I exaggerate only a bit. All of that opening could be covered by starting with the last four words and nothing would be lost. Instead, with the extended opening the audience is so far ahead of the scene they are falling asleep. They are just waiting for something to happen. Nothing is gained by all that preparation. Great actors might be able to milk that opening, but if you start with those last four words the audience is hooked and you are galloping into the scene.

Another important rule may be gleaned from this scene: the later in the scene you can start without losing anything, the better. In the long doctor-patient exposition, we could eliminate the first six exchanges. In any scene you are working on, if you find that you can start it at a point five or six or more lines further in, by all means do it. Keep shaving the opening lines until you have reached the vital point. Another of my quarrels with improvisation as a presentational form is with the time often taken just to find an opening.

We have all witnessed—and some of us have even participated in—an improvised scene where the exposition, the actual beginning of the scene, does not occur until the end. The actors flounder around for ages until they actually discover the opening, at which time the light man, who has been seeking an out point for three minutes, blacks the scene. We can illustrate this by again taking up the doctor-patient situation.

Start with two actors in a doctor-patient relationship. They are improvising, and they are titillated by the idea of a pushy, aggressive patient and a timid doctor. It's funny, right? So they trade clever ad libs for three minutes. The jokes are flowing, but there's no real subject matter, no real action, and the audience grows more dutiful by the minute. Finally, depending on how big their egos are, the actors realize they had better get off stage while the going's good, so they end the scene with the doctor prone on the floor, the patient with one knee on his chest saying, "Well, doctor, will I live or won't I?"

That scene as I described it can be funny, and the audience will laugh and some of them will think they have had a satisfying experience. But it is not as much as the actors could have given them or as much as they could have come away with. Yes, keep the bumbling doctor and the aggressive patient, but make a scene out of it where the humor is not about that particular silliness but about the whole notion of healing, or life and death, or the cost and quality of medical care, or whatever. You might even keep some of the same jokes, but if you do this as a scene, with something of significance happening between those two actors, everyone will have a better time.

Exercise: Openings
Divide the class into pairs. Give each of them a profession. Have them work on an opening that fulfills the
requirements of who, where, and the nature of the problem. Each pair presents its opening in turn, and the rest
of the class discusses the relative success of their efforts.
They are then either succeeded by the next pair or, if
the director feels it valuable, they repeat the opening
in line with the suggestions.

A clarification about openings: when I point out that the
more explicit the exposition, the better, I am not violating
the rule that showing is better than telling. In creating, we
rightly value the implicit over the explicit. The former is
more subtle, more intelligent, more artistic, more worthy.
Ambiguity is the soul of good work. It is more effective to
show than to tell. So strong is this notion of the superiority
of the implicit that for some artists it even carries moral
overtones. They feel that to be explicit is to pander to the
lowest common denominator of the public. This is valid when
it comes to the heart of the matter—that is, what the scene
is all about. But let's say you are doing a scene in which a
refrigerator is broken. And that broken refrigerator is causing a quarrel between a husband and wife. It does not detract from your art to explicitly say the refrigerator's broken.
It does not detract from your art to say explicitly that they
are husband and wife. It does not even hurt if the audience
understands that she wants out of the relationship. The implicit lies in how they deal with these "facts," and in the
actions that ensue. In our zeal to be allusive we sometimes
go too far and avoid the explicit, even when it is necessary.
Unless they have no bearing on the scene, the facts must

get stated in one way or another. Yes, we can find ways to open scenes in which the needed information is presented in an allusive context. But remember: the scene starts when the problem is engaged, and we must know what leads to that problem. The definition of exposition includes giving the necessary information. If it can be derived without baldness, great. But if I must choose between a bald statement that gives me the information and a delicate opening beat that does not, I will take the bald statement every time.

In the refrigerator scene, the characters' wants have nothing to do with fixing the refrigerator. It could be that one character wants the other to move out and is using the broken refrigerator as a ploy. The real mystery, the art, lies in the interaction between the characters once we know the refrigerator is broken and what they want from each other. That's when the mystery of creation in all its ambiguity starts. At that point we cannot be explicit or we will all go to sleep.

If you are made uncomfortable by bald exposition, rest assured that once you understand the needs of that opening beat and have dealt with it a few times, your creative impulse will lead you to be concise and informative and clever about it all.

Pre-planning in Writing or Improvising. "You can't improvise on nothing."—Charlie Mingus.

How much we, as improvisers and writers, should know or "set" about a scene before starting into it, how much pre-planning we should do, is a controversial question. Some disciples of improvisation, the true believers, feel it is a point of honor as well as aesthetics to go into a scene with no pre-planning at all. They feel they lose spontaneity by even thinking about the scene before they go on stage. Too often this leads to what I have already described: about the time you find out what the scene is about, the lights come down because you have been on stage a long three or four minutes.

I believe the opening should be planned, or at least that everyone should agree on the necessary information—who the characters are, where they are, and the nature of the problem. The heart of the matter—the action of the scene and the free flow of that action—is helped, not handicapped, by initial agreement. Searching for the agreement on stage leads to delay and actually fetters freedom. The time wasted in the longer doctor-patient scene could have been avoided if the two actors had agreed on the fundamental information. No significant artistry would have been lost by this pre-planning, and much gained. The amount of time spent in this way is usually less than that spent in floundering around, looking for an opening on stage. It frees the actors to cut to and explore the scene itself. After a company of actors goes through the pre-planning experience a number of times, they grow more comfortable with one another. A shorthand develops among them.

Group Scene Openings. In most group scenes on our stage, only one or two of the characters should be there at the opening—for a simple logistical reason. In a short scene with five or more characters of equal importance, if you open the scene with all of them on stage, it is difficult for the audience to sort them out, to learn who they are and their function in the scene. If they appear one by one or two by two, as justified entries in the scene, we can get to know them: a teaching scene with the students arriving and being greeted, a doctor's waiting room with the patients entering.

In the pre-planning of group scenes, the cast discusses

the point of the scene, and each member comes up with his or her own character and the wants of that character. If you do have everyone on stage as in, say, a political caucus, then it is important that each actor gets a chance to identify his or her character through a roll call or some such device.

The necessity of meeting and getting to know all the characters in group scenes imposes a slight variation on the conditions for openings that we laid out earlier. We need more time to get out all the information. It is well therefore to construct the scene so that there is some forward movement going on before the opening information is completely transmitted. This point is illustrated in the scene "Les Audiences" at the end of these notes.

Exercise: Full-cast openings

Divide the class into five- and six-member groups. Have them devise and present an opening scene that allows them, either by staggered entries or some roll-call device, to introduce each character.

After the Opening. What happens to a scene after the opening? We are now dealing with the mystery of creativity. This is where the characters play out their strategies for achieving the wants expressed in the opening. This is where "raising the stakes" enriches the events on stage. If this has been properly done, we have set the physical scene, identified the characters, and delineated their wants. One of the things that happens next is that each character plays out his or her strategy for achieving those wants. Against the background of the situation we developed through raising the stakes, this constitutes the middle section of the scene.

In the development process this is the period of exploration of the territory created by the opening. Let's return to the example we used before on the theme of borrowing money. In exploring the scene, once we have established the basic opening beat we can try out various themes: sibling rivalry, snobbery, etc. What would make the rich couple agree to the request? Blackmail? Guilt? Some sort of trade-off? What happens to the scene if we change the environment?

Here are a few general precepts to follow for our middle section.

1. Each subsequent beat after the opening must advance the action. We cannot stop to make lists or to get into arguments (I call them yes-no's). Actor 1: Tell me. Actor 2: No. Actor 1: Please. Actor 2: No way. Actor 1: I have got to know. Actor 2: Too bad, etc., etc. As to lists, there does seem to be a rule of three in comedy. How fat was he? 1. He was so fat that . . . 2. He was so fat that . . . 3. He was so fat that . . . Almost invariably a fourth will elicit fewer laughs.

2. We cannot stop to dwell on a peripheral beat merely because it is funny. When dealing with a scene, see what you can take away without hurting the flow, even if it means taking out a joke or a beat much loved by the actors involved. It all has to do with staying ahead of the audience. The biggest fights I have with actors occur when I try to take away one of their jokes. No matter what my explanation, their comeback is, "Well, the audience was laughing, wasn't it?" I patiently explain why the flow of the scene is hurt by the joke, even if it gets a laugh. Then I even more patiently explain the philosophy of scene construction. Then I appeal to their sense of ensemble and group solidarity. Finally and reluctantly I just say no.

In all dealings with actors, as a last resort you must insist on your no—but only as a last resort. Before that you modify, you suggest, you agree with qualifications. No is final. There is no graceful way to respond to it. "Yes, but" is better. Use "Yes, and" if possible. "Let's try it this way" sometimes works. I would encourage the same spirit among actors in their dealings with one another about the work. Restrict the word "no."

When and how to say no is important in building a company of cooperative actors. I believe that the most cynical among us is capable of and eager for commitment. Indeed, some of that cynicism stems from the fear that one is incapable of commitment. As a director you must assume that each of your actors is eager at some level to do the right thing. Find that level, whether it lies in pragmatically proving that each actor's fate is in the hands of his or her fellows, or in inspiring them as a community—if only for a moment, or ultimately by calling due what they owe to their art.

Point out to your actors that in the theatre we find a vocation, in the priestly sense of that word. Your life and work are not separated as you serve your community. Your existence does not divide into a nine-to-five working day split off from the rest of your life. In the theatre these are seamlessly joined.

Even if your actors wind up going to Hollywood and becoming rich and famous on the tube—and never learning how to act—while they are with you in this work they are embarked upon a vocation. Part of that is respecting your audience, your fellow actors, and your craft. Part of that is subduing your individuality in favor of the ensemble. Part of that is giving your all at every performance. Part of that is not saying no to your colleagues.

3. Show, don't tell. Whether it is a classic play or a review scene, the theatrical transaction is the same. On the stage a character is being portrayed with whom we identify. Therefore, at a remove, what is happening to that character is happening to you. Aristotle called it catharsis. But except for stand-up comedians, actors do not work directly on the audience; their relationship is to their fellow actors. Scenes do not work by making statements. The events of the scene as they illuminate the characters create the work. To deal directly with the audience (telling) is manipulative. To serve the work by preserving the distance between actor and audience (showing) makes it possible for the audience members to have a real experience that changes them forever. That is the power of art.

4. Pick no easy targets. The ultimate, most worthy target of this work is yourself—your own beliefs, icons, and shibboleths. It's easy to attack the Ku Klux Klan with their childish costumes and their unredeemed red-neckism, but to think of the Klan as an American phenomenon, to think of something in our own behavior that is parallel, is not to sanction the Klan but to portray the potential Klanism in ourselves. We do this by playing all of our characters—including villains—with reality and sympathy. Characters in a scene must speak in their own voices. In a current review a group of Americans sing a song that says, "We are ugly Americans and we don't give a damn about the rest of the world." Would an ugly American call himself ugly? No. People justify their positions in the name of goodness. Yes, the audience seems to like the song. It's a crowd-pleaser, but in my book it's unworthy.

To believe that our ideas are true and incontrovertible, that they represent the only path of truth, is to cut us off from change. Don't set up straw characters to destroy with the power of your truths. That's just preaching to the converted. And if you say the song should stay because it's interesting, I say they could drop their pants and it would be interesting.

Often the most fearsome people, people with ideas that are incredibly repugnant, are likable. To attack them properly, you must understand them. The very act of making the enemy human is to win. Your audience will be absolutely excited by it.

The big sins—racism, war, terrorism—are best portrayed in the small, in their effect on the everyday human situation. Some years ago a stage play and a film called *Oh, What a Lovely War* dealt with the horrors of World War I. By the time the third sign went up enumerating the thousands of dead, and by the end of the third scene which told me again that the generals were evil dunderheads, I really didn't care any more. If all the killing is depersonalized, the work is derelict. Make it small, human, individual. A call to action is propaganda; an invitation to an idea is art.

Tell the truth. Tell the truth. Tell the truth.

Looking for the Ending. Endings to scenes are often difficult to find. You get a good idea, get a scene going, only to find you cannot end the damn thing satisfactorily. In desperation you may bring in a new piece of information at the last minute—I call it the long-lost-cousin-appears-as-if-by-magic ending—or you may whomp up a variation of "It was all a dream." We often see these solutions, and sometimes the audience even forgives them, but I don't. Here is the magic formula, the alchemist's stone of the short, comic scene: if you can't find an ending, look at your opening.

That's where the scene needs work. If the opening clearly states the problem and the wants of the characters, the ending will follow. The problem stated at the opening becomes the problem dealt with at the end of the scene. Trace the progress of that opening throughout the scene to the ending. Connect the dots and you have completed the scene.

That the problems stated at the beginning of a scene are dealt with at the end does not necessarily mean that these problems are neatly "solved." It may be that a lack of solution, even the denial of the problem—a father refuses to acknowledge his son coming out of the closet, for example—is the point of the ending. Unfair to the audience is the tacked-on ending: the new information, the *deus ex machina* of comedy. This does not mean that the ending cannot be a surprise. Of course it can. But the surprise must be justifiable in terms of the beginning information. Otherwise it will be like a detective story that gave you no clues to the killer.

Auditioning for and Acting in a Review

It may not be necessary to discuss acting in a review as a separate category since we have been dealing with it right along. But there are more things to say about it, and if I repeat some points it will not hurt.

Auditioning: Stage Presence. The auditioning process is by its nature messy, unscientific, and imprecise. It usually enables you to find out who cannot do the work but not necessarily who will succeed. Yet it encompasses many important acting principles.

The first thing we are struck with when an auditioner

Deng Xiaoping (Tim Kazurinski, left) and his interpreter (Bruce Jarchow) enjoying the Soviet-American conflict at the height of the cold war.

enters is stage presence. It's there or it's not. Some people who walk out on stage are not necessarily skilled actors or will never be great actors—but they are riveting. They radiate a sense of ease, self-assurance, and focus. And this quality is not confined to the stage. Chicago's first Mayor Daley had it. This short, stout fellow would enter a room and all heads would turn to look at him—not because he was the mayor, but because he had it. When it comes to stage presence and The Second City, inevitably we talk about John Belushi. He too had it: confidence, ease, and aura. Often he was a pussycat, sometimes a monster. He had limitless appeal on stage and inordinate ambition offstage, but he was mostly a nice guy and a challenge to work with. Was he a good actor? Good, very good, not great. But he did have that stage, movie, and real-life presence to the highest degree. He had what every great personality, every great actor, every great achiever has: total focus. He was always and completely in the present moment, laying aside any self-doubts as to his powers or any questions as to his technique. To do almost anything well, from playing baseball to acting, that quality is necessary.

Baseball in fact has an old axiom: "Thinkin' is stinkin'." For the baseball player making a play, there is only the ball at that moment. If he thinks of form or mechanics, or the consequences of missing—if he is focused on anything but the moment, he errs. Similarly the stage forgives the actor nothing. If he feels even a shiver of doubt or anxiety, if he is watching himself in any way, the audience will sense it and be uncomfortable.

This ability to focus is separate from talent, though without it talent will be wasted. The large question is whether focus can be learned. I tend to think so, and for one reason. There is one role in which even the least charismatic of women becomes luminous, the deserved center of attention—the role of a bride. The bride marches up the aisle with all eyes on her, and she is totally in the moment of being a bride. She is, no matter how plain, yes, she is beautiful. And she is saying with her whole being, Yes, I am a bride and I am beautiful, and we look at her and we say, Yes, yes, she's a bride and she's beautiful. And that is stage presence.

I suspect that we all have the capacity to call up the bride in ourselves on stage or in life. Each of us must find the key to whatever it is that brings us to that point of total concentration and belief in ourselves. If we do we will become brides—that is, we will command the stage.

It cannot be done by simply adjusting physical movements, because it manifests itself in perhaps hundreds of unsubtle details. It is transmitted by the actor's subconscious and received by the audience's subconscious. Even Stanislavsky gave up on "emotional recall" as the path to the unconscious, realizing that emotions cannot be willed.

At a classical piano concert it goes like this. The lights go down and come up. Pianist A is worried about his performance. Dressed formally, he enters, generally from stage right, takes twenty-two steps, puts one hand on the piano, bows, and sits down. And the audience, not knowing why, is uncomfortable. Another concert: Pianist B is confident, eager to play. He is dressed exactly like our first player, enters at the same place, takes twenty-two steps, puts his hand on the same spot on the piano, bows, and sits down. This time the audience relaxes, certain they are in good hands. Nothing overtly discernible accounts for such a contrast. No radical differences are apparent between the two pianists. But obviously they are sending out signals at a subconscious level that we can decode and that they cannot control. We have learned, from the cradle, to "read" the subtlest signs of security and insecurity. Perhaps it is the relationship of the head to the rest of the body, perhaps the length and timing of the arm swings. Whatever it is, as an audience we take in these signals subconsciously as they are being transmitted—at a subconscious level—which is why you cannot teach stage presence through physical adjustments. It comes from within and has to be reached the same way.

Nevertheless there are various methods of reaching it. One way is to find what Viola Spolin calls a "point of concentration." Here is an example that can also serve as an exercise. Line up five actors on the stage facing the class. Say to them, "Just stand there while we watch you." They start fidgeting. They are watching the audience. They don't know where to put their hands. They don't know where to look. They are a nervous-looking bunch.

Now say to them, "I want you to listen to and identify the different noises you can hear." Immediately they forget about themselves; they concentrate on something outside and, lo and behold, become interesting. They identify the whoosh of the air conditioner, the crackle of the paper you were turning over, the ambient street noises, etc. They have a point of concentration, something to focus on that brings them into the present moment. They are no longer aware of their situation, no longer worrying about what to do or how they look. I think it was Elaine May who said that you should walk on stage as the only one who knows you have a pound of chopped liver in your pocket—unwrapped. All of this is aimed at eliminating the wandering mind, the nervous fears, the self-scrutiny. As you grow skilled, your point of focus becomes your character and the events of the scene.

Auditioning: Intelligence. Along with stage presence I look for intelligence and reference level. You can teach an intelligent person to act; you cannot teach an actor to be intelligent. It is that simple. I have a prejudice in favor of education. I tend to select people who know who Dostoevsky was. Our entire first company in the good old days could take any poet and make up a poem on any subject in that poet's style, be it T. S. Eliot or Andrew Marvell or Elizabeth Barrett Browning. But I also recognize that such learning may not be totally necessary for the work. Certainly today's actors are highly intelligent. But specifying intelligence as a necessary quality for this work is neither snobbishness nor elitism. First, at least some of your audience is bright, and you must have a dialog with them. Second, since we develop our own material and deal with politics, art, psychology, and human relationships, intelligence is mandatory.

Furthermore, in all theatre, and especially in our work, the audience puts itself in the hands of the actors and bestows upon them a certain authority. Blunders and ineptitude vitiate that authority and destroy trust and respect.

Play at the top of your skill. Play at the top of your intelligence.

Auditioning: Using the Environment. Using the environment means using the space around you. It means acknowledging the other actor. It means creating and using the setting you are in and the objects, real and imaginary, in that setting. It means using a costume or a prop you found backstage. Some actors have such tunnel vision that all they see is what they are talking about. But if you use a chair as a bed, if you use a hat as a statement, if you are not encapsulated in your own little world—well, that's a great clue to ability. The good people will do it automatically, even if they are untrained. They use everything that's there and they invent things that aren't there. If an auditioning actor does not use the environment, I lose interest.

One school of thought says, "They are nervous about auditioning for you, and you have to make allowances for that fact." Yes, but you're nervous on opening night, you're nervous the first time you do a scene, you're nervous at a job interview or on a date. But you carry on. Here is the situation, these are the rules. If you have the ability to fight through that nervousness and do your stuff, perhaps even use it to your advantage, that's what we are looking for. As it happens, I do give people second and third chances. But I also think that every part of the audition process, from the time you say hello through the time you finish on stage, is a test.

Of course, it's part of the director's job to help the actors succeed if they can. I try to make the audition an informal, friendly, low-pressure situation. For a Broadway show or for many professional theatres, auditions can be cattle calls. You have handed in your resumé and you sit around with dozens of other actors, competitors. Dozens have been there before you, dozens will come after you. When your turn comes you do your thing on stage in front of people you do not generally see—faceless, nameless arbiters sitting out there in the dark. Then a hasty "Thank you very much" and you are gone. I think it is important to say hello face to face, to be friendly and encouraging, to provide a relaxed, informal atmosphere for the auditioning actors. But in the end, they do it or they don't.

Auditioning: Other Qualities. Finally I look at their acting ability. Are they convincing in character? Do they enunciate? Overuse their hands? Are they "actory"? And a big one: Do they listen when the other person is talking? It sounds simple: listening. It amazes me on the professional stage how many actors do not listen to one another. You must not only listen, you must also be *seen* to be listening. And you must be listening in character, listening as that character would listen. And actors must make eye contact. Insist on that. These are elementary points, but we must not neglect them in favor of a witty mind or a fast thinker.

Alan Arkin says that when a scene fails it is often because you tried to do too much by yourself. You did not
listen enough. If you are really listening the scene holds the
audience even if nothing is going on for a while. If the other
actor talking to you is making eye contact and you are really
listening, the audience is content to wait for the next event.
If you are not listening, they are not listening. Just as when
you are not seeing something, they are not seeing it. Listen
harder. How do you listen harder? You listen harder.

Exercise: Auditioning and character work
**Divide the class into pairs. Set the scene: the informa-
tion desk in a large department store. One actor plays
the information clerk. The other enters five separate
times, each time in a different character, asks for an
appropriate piece of information, leaves, and *immediately* reenters as the new character. There is to be no
scene writing. Generally the dialog is one line each. The
point is to grab a character on the run, then run.
(Heaven preserve us from the little child looking for her
mommy, or the bent-over suppliant looking for the toi-
let.) After five characters, the two actors switch roles
and repeat.**

Character Work. Playing a character in review and playing a character in a regular play require different skills. In
some respects, in the areas of telling the truth, of "inhabiting" the role, the demands are similar. The differences lie
in the level of intensity at which the characters are played,
in the depth of portrayal, and in the amount of the author's
own person that is allowed to show through.

To play our characters at the same level of intensity we

would play Lear or Hamlet is, strangely, not to share with our audience, since we cannot in a short scene justify that intensity. And because we present very short scenes and must play many roles, we forgo some of the details that delineate our characters. In a play you have two hours or so to develop a character in all its nuances. You can proceed slowly and in depth, revealing facets of the character over time and in a number of situations. In our work we do not have that opportunity. We play a great number of characters, each for short periods of time. We must grab salient facets of the character. We must still truly observe and accurately portray, but in less detail and depth.

In our scenes we both remain ourselves and become the character. This means we wear our characters more lightly, donning them like costumes. More of the actor's own persona shows through. This is why the review form is unsuitable for tragedy. Tragic characters are intense. Tragedy has heroes. Tragedy is complex over time. These strictures effectively bar tragedy from our stage. And because we are the theatre of the everyday, dealing with everyday problems, our acting style is far from the tragic mode. If we were trying for tragedy we would achieve melodrama or, worse, pure sentimentality. But by and large many of our acting problems are similar to those in any medium. Because of the versatility involved, the skill level required is of equal order. And the necessity to portray your characters truthfully is the same.

Furthermore, all the systematic approaches to acting are applicable to our work. Stanislavsky works. The Method works. Everything works as well for us as for any other actors. All systems help focus and concentrate. In my view, however, whether in our work or on the classical stage, as one gains experience it is well to forget about them and confront the work without their mediation. If followed to the letter, they are ultimately reductive and limiting. True, some very good actors continue to swear by one approach or another. But when you examine their work, it is only a notional use of a few precepts that they bring to it. What they actually do is confront the work on its own terms.

Almost all the skilled actors I have encountered have a very strong mimetic ability. They are able to brilliantly imitate vocal and physical characteristics. Coupled with that mimetic skill is the instinct to minimize, to achieve the greatest results with the most economic means. They know that external characteristics do not constitute a character and that only by internalizing can they effectively communicate. I do not like to see young actors play old persons by bending over, quavering, and walking with palsied hand trying to control a quivering cane. I do not like it when young actors play little kids by assuming a goofy expression, speaking in a lisping, high-pitched voice, and bouncing up and down on stage. These are examples of externalizing, displaying certain clichéd characteristics of the characters. It is best in our work to suggest these things. Take your own age as the base and play a bit older or younger, and act with conviction within those parameters. Otherwise the acting is so externalized as to become an annoying caricature.

Theory and Practice: How an Actor Learns. Your actors should not be burdened by theory. Although we have laid down a great number of precepts, watchwords, and methodologies, I think they should be used only when you are confronted with the specific situations to which they are applicable. I do find it useful to discuss the pitfalls that actors should avoid and the temptations they should resist. You can inspire them with a sense of the history and honor of their vocation—always bearing in mind that the true learning process takes place not in class but on stage. Everything one can learn about acting in class is communicated in a few months. After that, the real learning takes place in performance.

Here is the actor's learning process as I see it. On stage the actors in the course of the work are sending messages to the audience. The audience sends back responses, many of them highly subtle. For example, there are dozens of kinds of laughter: forced, rueful, uncontrollable, even silent. Just so, there are many kinds of silence: awe, boredom, hostility, enthrallment. These messages and the responses to them—the subtle, important parts—are being transmitted at the subconscious level. The sensitive actors (we call them talented) make their offerings, receive and decode these responses, and then modify their next messages accordingly— that is, they change their messages to elicit the response they seek, or they store them for further use if they are effective. They are learning, on stage, what to do in order to effectively convey their messages to the audience. Through playing, and only through playing, they become skilled at doing this. This is learning from experience, which is always more profound than learning from precept. These reflexive transactions between the actor on stage and the audience constitute the true training area for the actors. No class can give them this, only constant work on stage in front of audiences. Class can teach a little about movement, diction, and interpretation, but all of this is compassable in a short time. The heart of the matter takes place on stage. You can learn to act without classes by being on stage. You cannot learn to act by classes alone.

Acting Mistakes: Indicating with the Hands. In a review, as in a full-length play, many of the same acting rules apply—and the same mistakes are commonly made: overuse of the hands, for example. You can always spot beginning actors, and sometimes even experienced actors who have not learned their craft, by their constantly moving hands. They are so eager to tell and so fearful they are not communicating that they constantly use their hands to reinforce to the audience what they want it to feel. In practice this eliminates the effectiveness of the hands as a tool for expressive gesture. It also makes the audience uncomfortable. If hands are in constant motion, they come to communicate nothing but the actor's ineptitude and insecurity. An old rule of thumb is never to make a gesture for its own sake. But all actors will say they are making a gesture for a purpose. I prefer "Reserve a gesture for an important moment." It preserves a syntax for hand use and keeps it as a tool. Under certain circumstances, stillness is a gesture too. If someone is delivering a piece of terrible news to you and you remain still, it is sometimes more effective than if you throw your hands up or weep.

As with most stage habits, the overuse of hands is hard to break. I have gone so far as to demand that actors keep their hands in their pockets for an entire scene—in rehearsal, of course.

Acting Mistakes: Indicating with the Face. The actor is a communicator, and that involves telling. But as we have noted, art and audiences are best served not by telling but by showing. The actor's task is to curb his or her inclination to tell rather than show. (This is true of every aspect of our work. Music should not tell the audience what to feel, text should not tell the audience what it means.) A more subtle problem than the overuse of the hands, more difficult to correct (after all, one can tie the actor's hands behind his or her back), is something I call "face acting"—indicating by overuse of the mouth, the eyebrows, or whole head gestures. Again the problem is caused by the anxiety to communicate. As with the overuse of the hands, the effect on the audience is eventually distracting.

A neat point about correcting these problems is the analogy between the directing process and the acting process. Correction involves showing, not telling. You cannot merely tell the actors; they must be shown or, rather, you must find ways to help them to show themselves.

For example, I had a problem with an actor in a Vietnam scene. He was telling away. He was "acting." His mouth was going, his face was moving, he was as expressive as a sob sister. I said, "I want you to play this scene all through without moving either your arms or your face." We had to stop several times, but when he finally got through it, lo! He achieved greater communication and showed and elicited more profound emotion when he was forced to work only with stance and verbal delivery than when he was indicating every feeling with his face. And he felt it. That was the turning point, he felt it.

Exercise: Faces and hands

Divide the actors into pairs. Have them play an emotional scene "normally." Now have them play the same scene either with immobile faces or with masks, and without using their hands at any time.

Acting Mistakes: Excessive Underplaying. One of the hallmarks of The Second City's work is underplaying, i.e., casual, "naturalistic," unemotive line deliveries. When you have a problem with a line or even with a whole scene that you think should be funny but is not working, it is most often solved by throwing the line away. Indeed, the hallmark of The Second City acting style has been underplaying. Except in the case of parody, we frown on rhetorical flourishes, hyperdrama, or excessive reactions. Nine times out of ten, throwing away the punch line is more effective than hitting it on the head. But there is a danger here: underplaying is too often confused with low energy. The bad actor who is imitating the seeming naturalness of the skilled actor indolently allows the words to fall from his mouth. In fact it takes more energy to underplay, not less. And it takes skill, art, and timing to throw a line away while sharing with the audience.

If you have two people talking quietly in a scene, they must nevertheless reach the audience member farthest away from the stage while convincing us that they are speaking quietly and in character. This kind of projection and sharing takes more focus and requires more control than does shouting. It is a most necessary part of the art. To be casual is to summon up more energy, not less.

In attacking indicating problems in general, the actor must learn just how subtle modes of communicating can be. Here are two people talking. They face each other head-on. The words they are to say are neutral (the weather, last night's game). Now they find they are in love. The head of one moves ever so slightly, almost imperceptibly upward as he addresses the other. Now the listeners turn slightly so that there is a shoulder interposed between them. Now the talker's head remains stationary. The mood has changed, and with the most economical of means, so economical that a single hand gesture would seem enormous. Once actors understand the power of the small—of stance, tone, volume, fast or slow delivery—they begin to realize the possibilities open to them for effectively communicating with minimum means. They can then skirt the dangers of excessive and prolonged indicating.

It is useful, in rehearsal, to play against the emotions called for in a scene: play affectionate by being distant, angry by being controlled, etc.

Exercise: Underplaying

Divide the class into groups of three. Place the rest of the group at the back of the theatre. Have each group play a scene as "casually" as they can with the rest of the class at the back of the theatre as audience, calling out when they cannot hear the group on stage or when they are losing their casual affect.

Acting Mistakes: Prolonging the Emotion or the Action. Another problem is the continuation of a mode or manner of expression past the point where you have communicated it. A scene needs to move forward constantly, for reasons more important than the need for variety or the potential for audience boredom. A delight of the work is in the unexpected that remains plausible. We must go beyond fulfilling audience expectation; we must stay ahead of them. Run-of-the mill plays and most television programs are content to achieve their effects by first telegraphing what is coming, then playing it out. Or else continuing in a beat long past the time when the audience has registered it. It is a refined form of telling, not showing. For the passive couch potato, this is fine. But when, as in life, the next moment is not anticipated, the living audience is truly engaged at the highest level.

Thus actions and the modes in which emotions are shown must constantly vary through the work. If the scene requires you to show the same emotion throughout, you must change the ways in which you show it. In life a person does not display a particular emotion in the same way over time. If you are sad you weep for a while, collect yourself for a while, try to ignore it for a while, etc. An actor preserving the same emotional response over a long time—and in our work that can be a matter of seconds—is diminishing his returns. To vary the way you show your emotion is not only dynamically desirable, it advances the story. Beginning actors have a great deal of trouble with this point. I ask them, for instance, to show anger by speaking very softly and quickly, then end with a shout. Pace is also a consideration here. Musicians know that beginners tend to play faster as they grow louder, and slower as they play softly. Exactly the same is true of beginning actors.

Any action or emotion that remains unvaried for even a short time becomes an audience distraction. If the scene involves a typist, the act of typing, if prolonged for more than a few seconds, will take over from the scene's content. The same is true if a character in a rocking chair proceeds to rock through a scene, or if an actor playing a drunk persists in staggering around stage, slurring his words. (Most real-life drunks expend considerable effort in trying *not* to act drunk—a much more interesting approach to playing drunk on stage.)

Exercise: Varying the emotion, varying the action
Divide the class into twos or threes. Start a scene that involves giving and receiving a piece of bad or good news. Vary the reaction at least four times during the course of the scene. Discuss with the class. Now play a scene where one or more of the characters is involved in an activity—typing, playing tennis, etc. Have the class call out when the activity is taking over.

Acting Mistakes: Ignoring the Environment. As noted in discussing the audition process, actors are often so intent on their actions that they forget to create the environment—an important, integral part of our work. This means the space in which the scene is played (indoors or outdoors), and the objects in that space. As noted earlier, we have no help from set designers; the design is entirely up to the actors. Directors are often not as diligent as they should be about creating and maintaining an environment, since the scenes often "work" without much attention to this point. But to enrich your scenes and more fully involve your audiences, you must drill, use appropriate theatre games, cajole, jaw, and keep insisting on the importance of what we call the "where."

Acting Mistakes: Acting from Memory. When actors in a run have repeated a role a great many times, their temptation is to play from memory rather than experience, which results in their parts being delivered mechanically. By their attitudes they tell the audience what to expect. What to do about it? Some directors advise reaching back for your original inspiration. I think that's too difficult. I focus on the event—that is, what is actually going on among characters on stage at any given time—which can be different every night. Deal with the events of the play as if they are actually happening, and happening for the first time. It is very much a part of being in the moment. Just accommodate the event. The director can help by introducing something new. When you place a new actor in a long-running show, the show sparks up. Everyone is having a new experience. You can achieve the same effect by asking the actors to do something new, something minute but different. This will lead the actors to play from experience, as they did when they initiated their roles.

We have all had the experience of seeing a scene that was brilliant the first time or two it was done, then the more the actors messed with it, the worse it got. What happened? In all of art, when you try to re-create from memory rather than reexperience, you are lost. In the theatre, whatever it was that made that scene work—the freshness of the relationship, the credibility of the acting—is no longer happening. The actors are merely re-creating what happened not as an experience occurring at that moment on the stage but from a memory, and the scene is doomed. In that situation, start with the basics and guide the actors away from repeating what they did before.

Acting Mistakes: Keeping the Character Constant. In every good scene the character must change—that is, he must have a realization that changes his view of the world and himself. (In great theatre works this is also what happens to audiences.) If it is a good scene, none of the characters can be the same at the beginning as at the end. This must be indicated by changes in attitudes toward one another, in acceptance or rejection of worldviews, and in actions that would otherwise not have been taken. As the characters learn more about themselves, their actions change accordingly. It is important that these changes express themselves as actions and not as statements. A kiss and its nature tell us more about what happened to the two people involved than the statement "I love you."

What does not change are the characteristics that go to make up the character. Shy or bold, quick or slow, friendly or diffident—these must be consistent through the scene. That kiss can be bestowed and received in character.

Blocking and Stance. There are two kinds of blocking: for function and for emotion. The director's job is to combine them. Functional blocking is movement in response to necessity: an actor must be stage-left at the end of a scene in order to make a costume change; someone has to follow someone else off. These functional needs must be accommodated, but you must also justify them emotionally. This is true for every move an actor makes on stage—getting up and sitting down, and getting up again; or moving toward another actor, or moving away, moving upstage, moving downstage. These movements relate to the events in the scene, to the character's feelings, to what one character wishes to communicate to another, and finally to variety within the scene.

The big moves, the macro blocking, should be saved for big emotions, for a shift in the energy of the scene from one character to another, for high emphasis. Generally the actors create their own blocking as they build their characters, to be cleaned up later. It feels more natural that way. Tell them what works and what doesn't rather than saying, "Go there now." Avoid giving blocking readings just as you should avoid giving line readings, unless that is the only way to reach a particular actor.

As important as the macro blocking moves are the micro, by which I mean the positions of an actor's body in relationship to another actor. Not only the distance between them but the relative positions of their shoulders, their feet, their heads, etc. As noted in the section on indicating, one of the most interesting things in acting is how much stance itself communicates: rhetorical stance, denial stance, hostile stance, welcoming stance. If I want to explain something to you, for example, I face you head-on, my torso leans forward slightly, I look you in the eye. I am friendly, teaching. If I shift slightly to my left, interposing my right shoulder between us, even with the same words a whole different emotion is expressed.

As important as it is, you cannot teach the actors how to stand. If the actor is free and in the moment, the body does it automatically. But you can pare away all the other reactions, confining the actors to stance alone. Most of the time this will show them how much they can communicate with micro stance changes, including such subtleties as relationship and status.

Exercise: Stance
Divide the group into threes. Have each team play a short scene. Now repeat the scene with the director from time to time calling "shift." On the word "shift," the actors must vary their stances (facing each other, interposing their shoulders, turning away, leaning in, etc.) and continue the scene with all the other elements remaining the same. Discuss.

One of the reasons there are no solid rules for blocking and stance is the subtlety involved. In a situation where someone is sitting and someone is standing, the person standing is not always of higher status. It may be just the opposite. The person sitting down may be secure enough to control the situation even sitting down, which makes his position stronger, especially if the standing character is fidgety or evasive. And sometimes getting up in order to achieve status indicates insecurity. It is not that simple, which is why it must come from within. The best you can do is to send the actor back to the source of the emotion. I usually take away the chairs halfway through a rehearsal because the easiest thing in the world is for the actors to sit there talking to one another.

Putting It All Together

Following is a six-person scene whose genesis and final form are fairly typical of the way the work proceeds.

The idea for the scene first surfaced in a short improvisation, in which a graphic artist treats the fourth wall as a curtain, and by drawing it reveals the picture he is working on: the audience. The notion of treating the audience's world, the "real world," as art and the stage world as reality tickled all of us. Since we needed a full-cast scene for the show we were rehearsing, I suggested that this idea was rich enough to work on with that goal. We started out with the artist and went through the process of raising the stakes.

The artist has a girlfriend.

They are living together.

She wants to get married.

He is a conceptual artist who has difficulty with the notion of selling his work, so he covers himself by not considering his paintings finished. And he does not want to get married. (Note the parallel between not letting go of his work and not getting married.)

He depends on his parents for money.

The intellectual danger to avoid in the scene is the temptation to denigrate conceptual art with easy laughs.

"Les Audiences"

Dierdre and Dexter on stage. Dierdre is bustling about preparing for guests. As the lights come up, Dexter is finishing pulling an imaginary curtain across downstage left.

DEXTER: Dierdre, I can't believe you invited my dealer over to see this painting. It is not even finished.

DIERDRE: Dexter, this is important. He's bringing a corporate art buyer and you are acting like a child.

DEXTER: I am not a child, you're a child.

DIERDRE: No, you're a child.

DEXTER: No, you are.

DIERDRE: No, you're a child.

DEXTER: You are.

[This is one of the few permissible yes-no-yes-no beats since it is a childish beat, and they get more and more childish while calling each other a child.]

DIERDRE: I think it is about time you sold another painting.

DEXTER: I sold one last year, and it wasn't even finished.

DIERDRE: Dexter, it shows a real lack of commitment to me, to reality.

DEXTER: What's that supposed to mean? I work in the world of reality all the time . . . this loft . . . our relationship. . . .

DIERDRE: Help me with these potato chips. *(Dexter, having lifted the cloth slightly on the painting, is examining a bit of it intently)* Never mind. *(Dexter's gaze fixes on his hand)*

DEXTER: Dierdre, have you noticed these striations on my hand?

DIERDRE: *(crosses to look)* I wish I could say it was stigmata, but it is just paint. Really, Dexter, I would like to see you sell a painting or two. I'd like to see a marriage happening, and it is not.

DEXTER: Why is that so important to you? Nothing will change with marriage. I am completely faithful to you. My friends screw around on their girlfriends all the time. I have never once screwed around on you.

DIERDRE: Dex, do not use your lack of motivation as an excuse for your monogamy.

[End of opening beat. We have established who they are, where they are, and a set of problems between them. He has trouble letting go of paintings, she wants to get married, etc. We also learn that his dealer is coming with a client to look at a painting that he claims is not finished. Now it's time to meet two more characters and, as we observed in discussing group scenes, it's desirable to meet the actors one or two at a time. While we still have some expository beats going on, as is typical of group scenes, these new characters are also advancing the scene.]

(The doorbell rings. Dexter crosses to answer.)
DIERDRE: Now remember, we want to sell a painting.

(Dexter opens the door, and his mother and dad, Bonnie and Rick Hall, enter. They are farmers, so dressed, including Rick's John Deere cap.)

DEXTER: Oh! Hey! Mom! Dad! How are you? What a surprise. You remember Dierdre, don't you?

RICK: Hello there.

BONNIE: Oh sure, and you're still not married—but I am not going to bring that up.

RICK: *(to Bonnie)* Okay, Bonnie. *(to Dexter)* Well, surprise visit, huh?

DEXTER: Yes, but I am glad you are here. Is something wrong?

RICK: We have got something we need to talk about right up front.

DEXTER: Sure.

RICK: Mom, back me up on this.

BONNIE: *(over Rick's right shoulder)* I'm right here, yeah.

RICK: *(to Bonnie)* Okay. *(to Dexter)* We got that letter from you last week asking for more money.

[The fact that Dexter is being supported by his father is the last bit of expository information.]

BONNIE: Yeah, the letter about the money, you know.

RICK: *(to Bonnie)* Okay. *(to Dexter)* Well, you know things have been pretty tight on the farm . . .

BONNIE: . . . Yeah, very tight lately.

RICK: *(to Bonnie)* Okay, doggone it. *(to Dexter)* We are not going to be able to send you any more money. Now, doggone it, it doesn't mean we don't love you and support what you are doing and such, son, because we do.

BONNIE: Oh yeah. We support you. *(to Dierdre)* He was such a sweet baby. Doggone.

RICK: We just can't send any more money. We drove all the way here in the pickup truck. It is parked right outside. You can come home and live with us, if you want. We'd like that. We can't send up any more money. That is right, isn't it, Mom?

BONNIE: Uh huh.

DEXTER: Why don't you just sell the farm? I don't understand.

RICK: Sell the farm?

[Now the stakes have been raised in a couple of ways. The pressure on Dexter to sell his work is intense. There is also some anxiety at the prospect of this farm couple being around when the sophisticated dealer and the buyer arrive. As an audience we begin to think that Dexter is a bit selfish, or at least so wrapped up in his art that he has lost perspective, so to speak. It is important that he not play the role abrasively. It is also important that the farm couple not play caricatures. The father is troubled by what he must do, and the mother is loyal but divided. Dierdre is a bit panicky, feeling that her hopes for the dealer-client visit are in jeopardy. The interplay here between Bonnie and Rick is an example of comedy that comes from behavior rather than jokes. On the page their dialog does not read as being funny, but in the playing, Rick's need for her reinforcement coupled with his impatience when he gets it, plus her eagerness to proffer it, result in appreciative audience laughter.]

DIERDRE: I am sure Dexter is joking, Mr. Hall, and besides it may not really be necessary. It is just that you have come here at kind of an inconvenient time. We have a buyer who's coming today to look at one of Dexter's works.

RICK: Hey, mister! You gonna sell a piece of art?

DEXTER: Well, I guess I have to now, Dad, now that you have pulled the cord of my life-support system.

RICK: We are here five minutes and he's already got me pissed off. Dexter, you tell me what we are supposed to do. I have been sending money up here for two years—never seen any of your art, except the one thing we use as a doorstop.

DIERDRE: Dex, I cannot believe you haven't shown your parents any of your work. *(she's rushing now, anxious to get rid of them before the dealer and client arrive)* We have documented all of Dexter's work. Before you leave, let me show you some of it. *(Dierdre speedily flips through an album)* Here's "Dog Boy," here's "Tribute," "The Bridge," here's . . .

RICK: Whoa. Whoa, what's the deal on "The Bridge"? What's all that around it?

DIERDRE: Oh, it was just marvelous. It is Dexter's tribute to the artist Cristo. What he did was to drape fabric over the whole bridge.

BONNIE: Why'd he do that?

DIERDRE: Well you know—it was an attempt to isolate a random moment of experience.

BONNIE AND RICK: Oh!

DEXTER: Come on, Dierdre. They are never going to understand it.

BONNIE: No, no. I got it sure.

RICK: Yeah, me too. But I gotta say, anybody who wanted to use that bridge would sure be pissed off. Come on, Mom, we ought to go home and throw a quilt on the John Deere and make some art. We'll see you later. Mom?

BONNIE: I'm coming.

(Bonnie, Dierdre, and Rick are still all at stage right when there is a knock at the door. Julian, Dexter's dealer, and Daniel Davis, the client, enter. Rick and Bonnie are left alone on stage right as Dierdre rushes upstage center to greet them. Dexter slowly makes his way toward the newcomers.)

DIERDRE: Julian.

JULIAN: Ah, Dierdre, I'd like you to meet Daniel Davis, curator of the art collection for Amoco.

DIERDRE: And this is the artist. Dexter, this is Mr. Davis.

DAVIS: Ah, Dexter. We've heard a great deal about you at Amoco.

DEXTER: Well, thank you. I have heard a great deal about your gas.

(Daniel has spotted Rick and Bonnie and walks over to them, extending his hand. Dexter, Julian, and Dierdre remain on stage right, and a double scene is played here with the focus shifting back and forth. This is done by one group becoming audible as the other, continuing to mime talk, becomes inaudible.)

DANIEL: *(shaking Rick's hand, limply)* Daniel Davis, Amoco.

RICK: How you doin'. Whoa, give me a real one. *(Rick gives Daniel's hand a good squeeze)* I'm Dexter's dad, Rick Hall. This is his mom, Bonnie.

DANIEL: *(kissing Bonnie's hand)* Charmed, madam.

BONNIE: Oh, how do you do? *(She points to Daniel's bent head and giggles. Daniel notices Rick's John Deere cap.)*

DANIEL: Ah, I see you work with John Deere. Fine company. Colleagues of ours. *(confidentially)* Not much of an art collection, I'm afraid. Tractors, not Titians. Ha ha.

(They continue in mime and we hear from the other side of the stage)

DIERDRE: I don't know why you won't listen to what Julian has to say.

DEXTER: Because, fundamentally Julian does not care about me or my art. He's a mercenary. That is his job. Right, Julian?

JULIAN: That's not true. I believe in your work, otherwise I wouldn't represent you. All I really need is for you to give me something to sell. Besides, you wouldn't believe some of the crap I have sold this guy.

(The focus passes to the other side of the stage)

DANIEL: So you are a farmer. How lucky. I always wanted to work with my hands.

RICK: You know, Mr. Davis, we have got a tractor at home with a quilt you might want to take a look at.

DANIEL: Oh that is very funny. Sort of a rural Cristo.

BONNIE: That's us.

(The three are laughing and jolly and getting along. The other three are glum and intense.)

DIERDRE: *(on a signal from Julian, crossing with some dispatch)* Mr. Davis, can I get you something to drink?

DANIEL: Ah, yes. Any kind of bottled water will do. Dexter, is the piece behind this curtain? *(indicating downstage)*

DEXTER: Yes it is, Mr. Davis.

DAVIS: Well, let's take a look at it, shall we? *(he reaches out to draw the curtain)*

DEXTER: *(panicky)* Mr. Davis, please don't do that. *(Daniel draws back in some alarm. Dexter recovers.)* I'm sorry. Look. The thing is, the work really isn't finished. Maybe if you came back next month.

DANIEL: Dexter, Dexter, Dexter. *(his upraised hand stops Julian who is about to protest)* I understand the artistic temperament.

RICK: *(to Dexter)* Whoa! What did you say?

DEXTER: Dad, just stay out of this.

[What became clear in rehearsal was the constantly shifting alliances developing in the piece. Julian and Dierdre and the parents wanting Dexter to sell his work. Bonnie and Dierdre looking for a marriage. Daniel, exotic to the parents and they to him. Dexter and Dierdre, now together, now at cross purposes. Dierdre and Julian against Dexter's procrastination and, as we shall soon see, everybody against Dexter.]

RICK: What do you mean it is not finished, huh? *(to Bonnie, who is tugging at his sleeve)* Don't do that!

BONNIE: I'm not.

RICK: Nothin's ever finished, is it, Dexter? Nope. No, sir. We got a birdhouse at home from when you were a boy scout—that's not finished yet. There's a Huffy three-speed all over the garage, and Mom cannot pull the damn car in there. Damn it! *(over his shoulder, to Bonnie)* Gimme a Rolaids!

BONNIE: *(handing it to him)* Right here.

DANIEL: On the other hand, I do not want to precipitate a squabble here. Julian, in future I would appreciate being invited to showings of artists interested in selling their work.

JULIAN: Daniel, I apologize. Let me . . .

DEXTER: Mr. Davis! Mr. Davis! I'm sorry, you're right. Please sit down. I'll show you the piece.

(All except Bonnie sit in a row facing the audience)

DEXTER: Mom!

(Bonnie hastily swallows a Rolaid, then joins the others.

Dexter pulls open an imaginary curtain from across the entire front of the stage. As he does so the house lights come up. The cast stares at the audience with open mouths. Together they lean forward in their chairs to get a closer look at the "work" (the audience). Together they lean back and look at one another, then together they lean forward again to look at the audience.)

DANIEL: Dexter, this is brilliant! *(rising to get a closer look, then sitting down)* This is astonishing.

RICK: Son, what the hell do you call this?

DEXTER: "Les Audiences."

[As noted earlier, this single idea of the audience as an artwork was the one from which we began the process of developing this scene. Everything else—the characters, the relationships, the progress of the scene—came from the process of "raising the stakes" plus the usual rehearsal process of trial and error.]

DANIEL: Dexter, this is glorious. *(rising)* In one work you have encapsulated the entire history of art.

DEXTER: You see, Mr. Davis, there are three hundred some people in the work. Friends, the homeless, honest, dishonest.

(Julian has been crossing back and forth from left to right)

JULIAN: Daniel, you'll notice their eyes seem to follow you wherever you go.

DANIEL: Yes. Dexter, do you realize what you've done here? You've expressed every artist's secret dream. You've turned the tables on your audience.

DEXTER: Yes, I know. That's the point.

DIERDRE: Dexter, I am so proud of you. It is a masterpiece.

JULIAN: Have you noticed, Daniel: all of humanity, every artistic period and style is represented in this one work?

DEXTER: That is true. Over here is a splash of the Renaissance in which I have depicted an example of every one of the seven deadly sins. Over there is my homage to cubism: the gentleman with the square head.

BONNIE: I want to see this.

DEXTER: Over there on the left.

BONNIE: Oh, yeah. It is square, is it not?

JULIAN: And those people back there on the right are definitely surreal.

DIERDRE: And that table with the older gentleman and the very young lady is certainly da-da.

DANIEL: Looks like sugar da-da. Dexter, would you mind very much if I entered the piece?

DEXTER: No, not at all. Go be art.

DANIEL: This is a long-held dream. *(Daniel walks down into the audience but keeps one foot on the steps)*

DEXTER: And now you're art.

DANIEL: Very nice, I think. *(he hops back on the stage)*

DEXTER: And now you're not. *(Daniel jumps back and forth from stage to audience, Dexter accompanying him verbally)*

DEXTER: And now you're art. And now you're not. Now you're art, now you're not. Art, not. Art, not. Art, not, art.

DANIEL: *(remaining in the audience and looking around)* Dexter, this is phenomenal.

JULIAN: Daniel, if you find the right woman in there you can reproduce art.

DANIEL: Ah, conceptual art.

DEXTER: Why don't you try it, Mom?

BONNIE: What?

DEXTER: Yeah. Go in there. Go be art.

BONNIE: Me?

DEXTER: Sure, why not?

BONNIE: Oh gee, I am not really dressed or anything. Well, what the heck. *(Bonnie walks into the audience)* Oh, God! *(to Rick)* Honey, I'm art. Do you see me?

RICK: *(laconically)* I see you.

BONNIE: Just making sure.

DEXTER: Oh, look out. There goes Dierdre. *(Dierdre walks into the audience, stage right. Julian, holding his nose, jumps in, stage left, as if he were entering a swimming pool.)*

DEXTER: Oh, look out. Man overboard.

JULIAN: *(waving his arms in swimming motion)* Come on in, the perspective is fine.

(Dexter and Rick are the only ones left on stage now)

BONNIE: Come on, honey. I am your nymph, calling you.

RICK: *(looks around)* This is bullshit! This isn't art at all. It is just a bunch of people sitting out there. Why don't you throw a quilt on them, huh? What's the point?

DIERDRE: No, Mr. Hall. They are not a bunch of people anymore. They've been transformed into art.

DEXTER: Don't bother, Dierdre. What did you expect? He doesn't want to open his mind. He just wants to criticize what his son wants to do. *(to Rick)* Why don't you try supporting me for once?

RICK: Settle down there, sport. Mr. Davis, you're the expert around here. What do you think of this?

DANIEL: *(pause)* I think this piece can make your son a very wealthy young man.

RICK: Really?

DANIEL: Yes.

RICK: *(takes this in for a moment)* Whoa, I'm art. *(he enters the audience)*

[The delivery of "Whoa, I'm art," provided a classic lesson in the effectiveness of throwing away the line. Because it was said matter-of-factly rather than punched or "delivered," it had enormous impact, especially coming after a pause. This would be true even if it were not appropriate to the character, which it is.]

DEXTER: And now my work is finally finished.

DIERDRE: No, it is not, it needs you.

DEXTER: No. No. No. I'm the artist. This is my piece, and it's finished.

JULIAN: Then we have no choice but to turn the tables on you. We are making you the art. We are the reality.

RICK: You're art now, son.

DIERDRE: Look, everybody. Dex is art.

JULIAN: Be a nude! Be a nude!

BONNIE: *(proudly)* My son is art!

RICK: Who wants to buy him? I'll bid forty bucks. *(goes into auctioneer's chant)* I've got forty, forty, do I hear fifty? *(etc.)*

(The group grows more and more clamorous. Dexter is agitated and angry. Finally he goes to far stage left and starts pulling the imaginary curtain across the front of the stage. The stage lights go down in sync with the curtain pulling. When the curtain is completely drawn, Dexter exits.)

DIERDRE: Dexter! Don't do that. Dexter, what about us? I promise it will be all right. I . . .

(Except for Dexter, the entire cast is now standing in the

audience completely disconnected from the stage. They look around for a moment in silence.)

BONNIE: Well, this isn't much fun.

RICK: So, what the hell do you people do out here, huh? *(fast fade to black)*

[Because of the logistics of the scene as well as its content, I ended the first act with it. When I first showed it to a workshop, some participants suggested I had violated my own rule about the end flowing from the beginning. It may seem that way, but I do not believe it is. Right from the beginning, Dexter's problem of not being able to commit is the pivot of the piece. It is established in the opening and runs through the entire scene as the pervading theme. At the end he remains unable to commit, even to his art.

What I love most about the scene is how cleverly it deals with the questions of what is art and what is reality. Audiences were enthralled with all the transformations of reality. They were with it all through. The scene was brilliantly acted without a hint of playing to anything but the reality of the characters. The actors avoided the temptation for caricature.]

Index

A NOTE ON THE AUTHOR

Bernard Sahlins was born in Chicago and studied at the University of Chicago before he turned to the theatre, co-founding The Second City in 1959. He has won the Sergel Prize for playwriting, several Joseph Jefferson Awards for directing, and the Alumni Achievement Award from the University of Chicago for his contributions to the theatre. Mr. Sahlins also co-founded the International Theatre Festival of Chicago, and has produced television specials for HBO, Granada Television, and CBS. He was executive producer of the SCTV show in Canada. He also edits, with Nicholas Rudall, the Plays for Performance series published by Ivan R. Dee. He lives in Chicago with his wife, Jane.

Made in the USA
Monee, IL
14 November 2020